I0572223

Twenty-five years *one fellowship*

Twenty-five years *one fellowship*

A history of the Lake Macquarie Branch
of the Fellowship of Australian Writers, NSW

Editors

Pam Garfoot, Sandra Joy, and Linda Visman

Lake Macquarie Branch of the
Fellowship of Australian Writers

Title: Twenty-five years, one fellowship

ISBN: 978-0-646-72360-0

First published in September 2025 by the Lake Macquarie Branch of the Fellowship of Australian Writers, NSW.

www.lakemacfaw2.wordpress.com

A catalogue record for this work is available from the National Library of Australia

Cover design by Leanne Deering and Eva Geerling

Cover photo by Leanne Deering, at Stockton NSW

Other Lake Macquarie FAW titles:

978-1-876409-63-0	Beneath the Surface (paperback)
978-1-876409-49-4	Beneath the Surface (e-book)
978-0-909497-05-7	Beneath the Surface (large print)
978-0-909497-90-3	Out of the Shadows (paperback)
978-1-876409-05-0	Out of the Shadows (e-book)

Contents

Introduction

Many of us feel as if the year 2000 was only yesterday. It can be a shock to realise that a quarter of a century has passed since everyone entered 'the new millennium'. Well, it has been 25 years since the Lake Macquarie Branch of the Fellowship of Australian Writers (NSW) was formed, and those of us involved with the group are equally amazed that so much time has passed.

When members realised that a **significant** milestone was approaching, we decided that we needed to mark the achievement with some sort of celebration (planned for the latter half of 2025) and, as is in keeping with our group's aims, a publication of some sort. This anthology is the outcome of that decision.

Twenty-five years, one fellowship aims to offer both a history of our group and a taste of the creative writing that we do. It contains factual articles about our group's history, activities, goals, and achievements, as well as poems and short stories that reflect more loosely on these things. An array of photographs taken by many people over the group's life illustrate the anthology.

Additionally, we hope that this history will offer an insight into local voluntary groups like ours, each contributing to the lifeblood of Australia's creative arts activities. There is no doubt that local writing groups help to foster numerous aspiring and accomplished writers, each of whom add to our nation's wonderful creative output.

We have drawn upon the group's records – meeting minutes, internal newsletters, photographs and other bits and pieces – to write the articles. Unfortunately, because we are writers rather than record keepers or archivists, the records are not complete. However, they come close to providing a fairly comprehensive picture of the group's last 25 years.

We are immensely grateful to the group's members, both past and present, who have contributed to this anthology.

It was our aim that as many of them as possible be represented in *Twenty-five years, one fellowship*, making it both an entertaining and an accurate account of the Lake Macquarie Branch of the Fellowship of Australian Writers (NSW).

Editorial Committee

Pam Garfoot, Sandi Boyd, Linda Visman

Where do I go?

Linda Visman

When I want some help with writing,
about making it exciting
or interesting – or just real,
I give a shout to those who know
what writing's all about.
Or if they don't they'll help me find
an expert in a book or, mostly now, online.
They also give me great support
to keep my writing going
when it has started faltering
or it simply isn't flowing.
They'll critique my words and give advice
and do it with a smile.
So who are these who give a hand
and go the extra mile?

They are the wonderful members of ...
The Lake Macquarie Branch of
The Fellowship of Australian Writers.

Section 1

Why we write

We write to understand, to connect, to be heard. This section shares what writing gives and demands of us – revealing the personal rewards, quiet struggles, and deeper motivations that keep us coming back to the page.

The start of LMFAW

Rina Robinson, written in 2007

At the end of June 2000, I was asked to meet with Anna Scott who had recently come to live in Toronto. Mel Davies, who had joined me to run the writers' group for Toronto U3A, had met Anna earlier and one of them had suggested the formation of a branch of FAW in Lake Macquarie. Mel knew that I had belonged to the Newcastle Branch of FAW and that before that I had been a member of Manly (Sydney) FAW.

We three decided that, if there was sufficient interest, we would go ahead with the idea and we met again several times for discussion. We put an advertisement in one of the local papers.

The first public meeting was on 13 August 2000 at the Multi-Purpose Centre, Toronto, and there was a very good roll-up on that Sunday afternoon. Several members attended from the Pencil Orchids, a group with whom Anna had been associated before moving to Toronto. They were most encouraging and gave many tips on how to run a new writing group. This led to a decision by the people present to form a new group and to call it Fellowship of Australian Writers, Lake Macquarie Branch. It was to be open to anyone interested in writing in any of the surrounding districts.

The first meeting of this new branch was on Sunday 10 September 2000 at 1:00 pm with Anna Scott as President and me (Rina) as Vice President. Many new members brought their work, and we were divided into small groups to read and critique.

During this meeting there was also a discussion, and it was found that Sundays were not convenient for some people, so the date of the next meeting would be Saturday 7 October at 2:00 pm, with the committee meeting one hour earlier at 1:00 pm.

Very soon after that, a small group was formed of some members who were keen to have weekly get-togethers. The group met at Marie Henery's house on Saturday mornings and one took one's lunch and stayed until 2:00 or 3:00 pm. We had writing exercises and read and critiqued each other's work. The group was called Marama, and the name was made up of the initial letters of first names of the members of that first day. One of those attending was Alice Sinclair who became our second President when Anna Scott moved to Victoria.

All this seems long ago but is not so long when one thinks of the years that the FAW has been in existence and the many authors who have benefited from its conception.

on writing

Irina Frolova

since the days I learnt
to use pen and paper
I have tried to weave
a net of cursive letters

catch the moment fluttering
before my eyes
make it stay a little longer

I have tried to grasp this
restless world it will move
me with it will turn
me upside down

come to learn
I can only grasp
my pen and paper

so I make my countermove
and turn myself
all out

The LMFAW committee – teamwork from the outset

Pam Garfoot

According to the Constitution of the Fellowship of Australian Writers NSW Inc., under which our group broadly operates, the committee exists to undertake activities that are 'necessary or desirable ... for the proper management' of the group. That's a fairly formal way of saying that the committee makes things happen for the general membership of the group.

A successful organisation owes much to the effectiveness of the people who run it – that is, to its committee.

Our group has been lucky to have experienced many years when members were prepared to take on committee positions and offer something to help the group. From the very outset of our branch's existence we have had a committee, consisting of people who have volunteered their effort and their time (sometimes lots of both) to keep things running behind the scenes. And all for the love of writing.

The committee has collected our fees, responsibly managed our finances including the payment of bills, arranged regular meetings in appropriate venues, planned workshops and other activities, convened writing competitions, and focused on helping us all to become better writers. So, we need to take a more thorough look at the things the committee has done over the 25 years of its existence.

Following are just some of them.

Our first decade:

After the first 'packed' public meeting in August 2000 when the branch was formed, the group met for the first time as an FAW branch the next month, in September. A committee was formed with Anna Scott as President, Rina Robinson as Vice President, and other members in committee roles.

From the start the focus was on 'guest speakers, workshops, feedback and input from fellow writers'. It took a little while for processes to get sorted, but before the end of 2000 meetings had begun, a venue had been secured (the Toronto Multi-Purpose Centre), membership fees set, a newsletter (known then as *Macquarie Muse*) issued, and workshops planned. The committee was active and motivated.

Having started out devoid of all funds it soon became clear that fundraising and publicity needed to be added to the focus of the committee's activities. After the first year of operation the group had just $260 in its bank account. Much attention was devoted to conducting raffles and undertaking publicity activities designed to attract new members. Approaches were made to several local publications (including the *Lakes Mail*, the *Newcastle Herald*, and other smaller newsletters and bulletins), as well as local radio stations and television channels to carry publicity and notices about the group.

Small sub-groups were formed to critique members' writing (sometimes with a focus on specific genres such as poetry or non-fiction) but often, in the early years, these fizzled despite the enthusiasm of members.

Leading the group throughout these times were several active presidents including inaugural president Anna Scott, followed by Alice Sinclair, Nola McCarthy, Wendy Alexander, Beth Parnaby, Terry Colling, Lis Gerrard and Sophie Bush.

Other members whose names crop up continually in meeting minutes and who held various positions include: Rina Robinson, Janine Henkel, Jeanette Brewster, Michael O'Callaghan, Jo Tregellis, Meryl Harris, Marie Every Burns, Joy Wheeler Garland, Tony Mays, Keith Davey, Linda Visman and Gail Hennessy.

In the early years the Lake Macquarie FAW was asked by the Hunter FAW to assist it by running the Denis Butler writing competition and this resulted in some addition to the group's finances. However, by the end of 2005 funds were little more than double what they had been four years previously. The costs of producing the group's *Macquarie Muse* newsletter (largely its external printing, plus postage costs) continued to draw heavily on the modest funds.

Some of the tasks that fell to the committee to organise included both the important and the mundane: coordinating fire drills, preparing member badges, preparing a list of members, making members aware of etiquette when guest presenters were speaking (directing all questions through a chairperson, and deferring them until the end of the presentation), planning the group's ever-popular Christmas

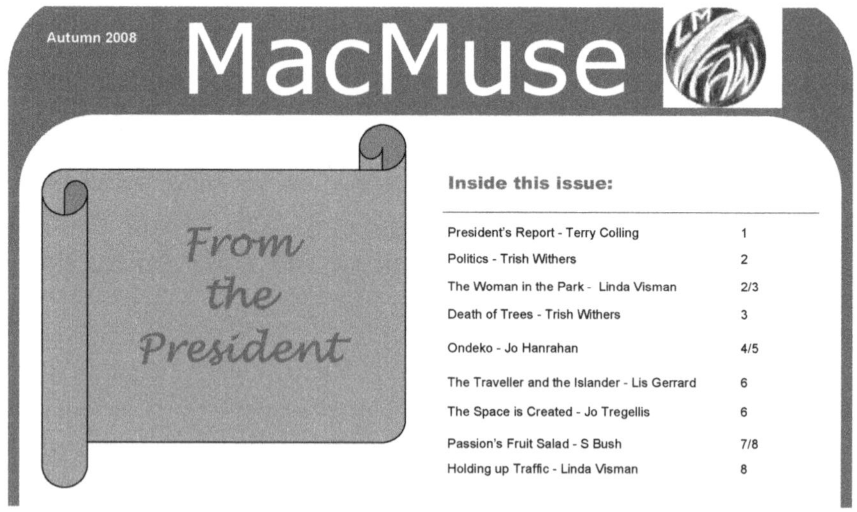

celebrations, ensuring the production of *Macquarie Muse* (which changed its title to *MacMuse* in 2006) and giving consideration to holding a writing festival.

Indeed by 2007 plans for a writing festival were well underway. However, having also been asked to host a Poetry on Wheels event (the 15th such annual touring event, initially organised by the Poets Union of Australia) the committee decided to throw its weight behind this poetry event instead. Despite considerable efforts going into Poetry on Wheels it was not the strong success members hoped for.

Critique sessions were successfully re-established in 2008 under the guidance of Linda Visman and Jan Mitchell. With regular leadership and the setting of some simple guidelines for operation, the critique process gradually became one of the most-valued aspects of our group. However, ongoing discussions reflected the group's uncertain and fluctuating approach to whether there should be different critique groups for different genres (for example, poetry, fiction, and non-fiction).

Publicity work continued to be a focus as the group approached its tenth year. A new logo was designed, although ultimately use of the FAW(NSW) logo was agreed upon. An information brochure was produced for distribution around the region. An email account was established, and a Yahoo group set up (though this was not long in operation). At much the same time as our group was actively promoting itself in this way, members were concerned to hear that FAW(NSW) might fold due to lack of people willing and able to take up roles.

By the time the group had been in operation for **ten years**, its financial position was becoming stronger – thanks in large measure to the promotional and organising work of committee members.

The group's bank balance routinely topped $1,000, allowing for greater scope in operations. Committee members were turning their attention to planning some sort of writing festival (a Writing Expo), which was eventually held in 2011 at the Toronto Library and praised for its vibrancy and success.

Several members by this time were exploring self-publishing, generally through use of what was then known as CreateSpace (now known as KDP or Kindle Direct Publishing). At the same time it was acknowledged that the group needed to provide sound support for less experienced writers who were not even close to publishing their own pieces – something that generally remains true to this day.

Our second decade:

Moving through our second decade, some of the 'old hands' moved on to other things, but the group continued to find new members and new stalwarts to be on the committee. Presidents over this period included Jan Mitchell, Linda Visman, Alison Ferguson and Kristen Mair, all of whom remain in the group today. Other office holders included Christina Batey, Neridah Kentwell, Jeanne Rigby, Helen Marshall, Vicki Norton, George Graves, Glenys Buselli, Christy Lutz, Cate Plink, Elizabeth Hunt, Elizabeth Horwitz, Heather Lang, Tony Lang and Pam Garfoot.

Some changes during this period include moving our meeting date to the second Saturday of each month, transferring our bank account to a different bank, holding a second critique meeting each month, and holding our AGM later in the year (June and, later, July). Fees were increased from $40 to $45 per annum, and outside speakers for general meetings were offered a slightly increased gift. These changes represented the natural progression of a group seeking to anchor itself in a changing and more costly world.

A Writers Showcase was held in August 2013 at the Warners Bay Performing Arts Centre. Several prominent local writers participated and the local member of NSW Parliament, Greg Piper, opened the proceedings.

Much work was done by the committee and the showcase organisers to get the showcase up and running, so it was disappointing to find that the event ran at a small loss.

Even in the face of this loss the group's finances remained secure, at above $1,000, and membership numbers were also sound (21 members).

In 2014, some committee members hosted a stall at the Toronto Spring Fair, resulting in some new interest in the group. Planning began for a panel presentation at the Newcastle Writers Festival in 2015. The presentation was generally considered successful, though it was acknowledged that better planning and a clear shared objective would have improved the process.

Lake Macquarie Branch, Fellowship of Australian Writers (FAW)

Local Writers Showcase

Saturday 31st August 2013 at Warners Bay Performing Arts Centre

PROGRAMME

TIME	*WRITER*	*GENRE*
11.00am	Welcome from Lake Mac FAW	Linda Visman, President LMFAW
11.10	**Official opening by Greg Piper, MLA,**	**Member for Lake Macquarie**
11.20	Group presentation with: Magdalena Ball Jaye Ford Judy Johnson Beryl Mullard	 Poetry; Fiction; Non-fiction Psychological thrillers Poetry; verse novel; novel Local History
12.15pm	**LUNCH BREAK**	
12.35	Rina Robinson	Short story, Poetry
12.40	Lachlan Ness (Tony Lang)	Non-fiction: Memoir & stories
12.55	Kaz Delaney (Kerri Lane)	Young Adult Fiction
1.15	Carol Wylde-Browne/ Claire Shields Wangi Sailing Club	Local History
1.30	Carol Heuchan	Poetry & Performance
1.50	Jean Kent	Poetry
2.10	Jan Mitchell	Biography & Memoir
2.20	Debbie Robson	Fiction – historical & contemp.
2.40	Christina Batey	Young Adult Fiction
2.50	Linda Visman	Young Adult Fiction
3.00	Karen Davey-Phillip	Non-fiction: Raising children
3.15	Linda Brooks	Non-fiction, Fiction (children's & adults), Publishing
3.40	Elizabeth Horwitz	Getting started in Writing
3.55	Close and thanks	Linda Visman

All speaking authors will sign and sell their books on the day. Others authors will not be speaking, but will attend, and will sign and sell their books.

Julie Brayshaw (Historical Romance)
Meryl Harris (Children's chapter books)

Several authors have kindly donated books for the Lucky Door Prizes:

Annie West (Romance); Pam Garfoot (Family History)
Linda Visman (Y.A.)

Lucky door prizes will be drawn from entry tickets throughout the day.

It was around this time, midway through our second decade of operations, that we began to explore the creation of a website for the group. We needed a site where permanent information about our operations could be posted.

A more significant happening, though, was the fact that some divisions began to develop within the group. Some members felt that operating under the auspices of the

FAW(NSW) brought few benefits and unnecessary costs. Two members resigned from the group to start an alternative, more casual group, and for a while some other members straddled both groups.

It was a troubling time for various reasons but, ultimately, our group's membership remained strong.

Our website https://lakemacfaw2.wordpress.com/ went live later in 2015, thanks to the work of Pam Garfoot and Alison Ferguson. The website structure was simple but clear, with the updating content being mainly notifications of upcoming meeting and workshop topics.

We received notification, about this time, that our proposal had been successful to have founding member, Rina Robinson, honoured with a Distinguished Service Award (DSA) from the State Executive. Her well-deserved award was presented at our annual Christmas celebration by Maureen Kelly, the State Honorary Secretary. The following year Linda Visman also received a DSA – again, very well-deserved.

In 2016 our group committed to corporate membership of Hunter Professional Arts Inc. (HPA), a Newcastle-based organisation supporting the arts in the wider area. LMFAW member Elizabeth Horwitz was also president of HPA and became a conduit between the two groups.

HPA Magazine was, for some years, a place where our members could regularly have material published for a wider audience.

A new era dawned for our Alice Sinclair Memorial Writing Competition in 2016. Online payment of entry fees and a wide publicity program resulted in increased entry numbers although it was not until future competition years that this began to positively impact finances.

In 2015 and 2016 committee members had some concerns over the group's dwindling funds. Consideration was given to seeking funding through the local council grant process. However, further investigation revealed that grants were essentially awarded for an organisation's 'event' activities (not for ongoing operations). Furthermore, not actually being an independent legal entity in its own right precluded LMFAW from applying. Fortunately, by late 2016 our bank balance was again solid ($1,591).

The year 2017 was a stable one for the group. May saw the Committee organise something a bit different for members: a successful bus excursion to Pokolbin in the Hunter Valley, with the focus being on getting writing inspiration.

Later in the year FAW(NSW) began an involvement with Seniors Card NSW in its Seniors' Stories Competition. They sought our group's contribution to help support this involvement. Each year from this point onwards LMFAW members (in particular Cate Plink, Jan Mitchell and Linda Visman) have contributed their writing expertise, by running preparatory workshops, helping to convene the competition, and assisting with judging.

In 2018 the Committee continued to focus on familiar ground: publicity and promotion, competitions, and finances. Some members participated in Toronto's Senior Lifestyle Expo in August, again eliciting some new interest in our group. The Alice Sinclair Memorial Writing Competition was held again, drawing 66 entries (much the same as in 2016) and there was modest growth in the group's funds.

Our group once again participated in the Newcastle Writers Festival in April 2019. A panel of members (all of whom were also committee members) presented on 'The Making of a Book' which proved timely with self-publishing being an ever-growing route to publication. The panel presentation once again drew a positive response from the audience.

Committee business often focused on planning meeting topics and possible presenters during 2019. As ever, committee members were keen to ensure that a wide range of topics and genres were addressed at general meetings so as to cater to the varied range of interests and skill levels amongst LMFAW members. In this year alone, topics were as disparate as writing thrillers, point-of-view, microlit, writing haiku, and self-publishing.

About this time a suggestion had been made, not for the first time, that our group produce an anthology of members' writings. A small and dedicated sub-committee was formed to progress the idea and this led to 2019 being a year which focussed on 'all things anthology'.

The sub-committee set a '*Beneath the Surface*' theme. Several relevant workshops were held (brainstorming story ideas, deciding on point-of-view, and writing author biographies) and a rigorous process of critiquing the pieces which had been submitted for inclusion began. The sub-committee insisted on two critiques for each piece, resulting in work of very high quality being included.

By the end of the year the group's anthology, now formally titled *Beneath the Surface,* was coming together well. An evocative cover inspired by the lake and water environment of Lake Macquarie was designed, and a meticulous editing process was underway. Although it had been hoped to publish before the end of the year, copies were not delivered until January of 2020.

The committee and the anthology's editorial sub-committee were hopeful of having a book launch in conjunction with the 20th anniversary of the group sometime during that year. However, they did not bank on the outbreak of a world-wide pandemic in 2020. As a consequence of the pandemic, both the launch of *Beneath the Surface* and the celebration of the group's 20th anniversary were low-key affairs.

The year of 2020, hampered as it was by isolation and lockdowns, proved nevertheless to be a good one for LMFAW. The committee went to considerable effort to keep the group together and to offer activities that members could participate in from home (most notably Zoom meetings and critique using Google Drive). Many Australians found that their unexpected 'confinement to quarters' meant they could explore activities like writing. So perhaps we shouldn't have been surprised when the Alice Sinclair Memorial Writing

Competition drew a record number of entries (182 in total). Our finances had never looked so good.

Committee meetings (and, of course, the Annual General Meeting) presented some challenges during 2020 and the following year but, somehow, we got through it all.

We survived the pandemic period with membership numbers steady and the continuation of an engaging schedule of events for members. It was a boost to the group's spirits, though, when in March 2021 we received a Lake Mac Award in the Artist and Creator Category of the awards made by our local council, and our group was mentioned in State Parliament by local MLA Greg Piper.

Our third decade:

As we began our third decade of operations and moved past the pandemic challenges, membership numbers remained strong, on one occasion rising up to a dizzying high of 39 members. At one point at least we had the highest membership numbers of any branch in FAW(NSW).

Despite the growth of our group, our committee positions were largely held by familiar names, apart from the addition of Bronwyn MacRitchie, John Franks, and Olga Korlevic in various Committee roles. The sequence of presidents saw Pam Garfoot, Irina Frolova and Sandra Boyd take on the role.

Stable membership numbers and the continued growth of the Alice Sinclair Memorial Writing Competition ensured very sound finances. We have been able to invest in some modest equipment (including a PA system and a pull-up promotional banner) as well as inviting outside speakers several times each year.

For some years it had been suggested to the committee that eager writers living on the eastern side of Lake Macquarie were unable to participate in LMFAW meetings. Although many might wonder at this, the eastern side of the lake is quite a distance from the western side.

Once again, we explored options for offering some sort of writing group support (either a new group or an extension of LMFAW) for these writers. We initiated some 'Eastlake' meetings, largely focused on critique, at Charlestown Library. Take-up was not high and, despite some valiant efforts, it proved impossible to sustain support for such a group without considerable work by committee members who were already working at capacity.

As always, committee members were eager to celebrate the successes of both the group and its members. A small 21st birthday celebration, complete with a cake cut by founding member Rina Robinson, was held in 2021 since one had not been possible the previous year to celebrate our 20th.

As we moved into 2022 the committee again focused on the biennial Alice Sinclair Memorial Writing Competition, endorsing as its theme as '*out of the shadows*'. It was agreed that the shortlisted stories and poems from the competition be published as the second anthology of our group. Ultimately all but one of the shortlisted writers agreed to the publication of their pieces.

The *Out of the Shadows* anthology was published in 2023.

In August the 100th issue of our internal newsletter, *MacMuse*, came out. *MacMuse*'s editor, Linda Visman, did a wonderful job of gathering relevant pieces for this edition and including a wealth of historical detail. Another achievement for the year was our role (led by member Joan McCarthy) in the 'Awe and Wonder' project convened by Lake Macquarie Libraries and focused on writing, art and creativity.

Issue 100

A Publication of Lake Macquarie Region
Fellowship of Australian Writers
August 2022

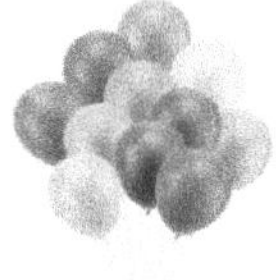

Macmuse turns 100!

A Short History of MacMuse

Linda Visman

Some time after Lake Macquarie FAW held its first official meeting in June 2001, the members decided they needed a newsletter. I don't know who suggested it, or when it began, as the earliest extant copy is dated June 2004, and the next is July 2005. However, we do know that it was issued quarterly as a printed document for several years.

The newsletter was known originally as the ***Macquarie Muse***. At some stage between July 2005 and the summer issue of 2006-2007 (which is when my collection of printed copies begins), the members decided to put the two original words of the title together. I then became ***MacMuse,*** a much more succinct name and a great play on the first. The autumn 2008 issue was the first to bear that name.

The main aim of the newsletter seems to have been to share members' writing. In the early years, from what I can see, there was little extra in the way of information sharing. MacMuse has gradually moved on from there and to become an informative newsletter. As well as showcasing members' writing it also contains articles about writing, grammar and sentence construction, book and movie reviews, and a great deal more. Later in this issue, you will see a list that shows just how many aspects of writing assistance and writers support our MacMuse can and does share.

In 2008, under the editorship of Linda Stewart, MacMuse gradually became digital. It was also available in printed form for those who couldn't access a copy via email. Within about three years, MacMuse was almost completely electronic. Also in 2008 a new LMFAW logo was added to the 2007 masthead (see info inset later in newsletter)

In 2009, under Linda Stewart's editorship, MacMuse became a bi-monthly production, and has continued to be so ever since.

1

In 2023 another of our longest-serving and most hard-working members, Jan Mitchell, received a DSA – much to her surprise. Three members have now received these awards. A further milestone was reached in January 2024 when Rina Robinson, still a much-valued member of LMFAW, celebrated her 100th birthday.

Sandra Boyd, taking on the role of president in 2023, initiated a process of recording the roles and responsibilities of each committee member. This has been harder than it sounds and a 'procedures manual' is still incomplete. It has been an eye opener for us to realise just how much is involved in keeping our group afloat and on track.

The past 25 years of committee operations have certainly been a mixed bag. On the deficit side, committee members would probably agree that they are disappointed in being unable to attract more members to take on office-bearing roles. Attracting members with specifically-needed skills (such as financial record-keeping, and website design and maintenance) has been even more difficult. Thankfully our already stretched committee members have 'gone the extra mile' to keep things rolling along but one day this may no longer be possible.

On the positive side, committee members would probably agree that serving with a strong group of like-minded people has forged wonderful friendships and given them a great deal of satisfaction. Guiding LMFAW through 25 years, including through a challenging pandemic, has been hard but rewarding.

Work life balance, what work life balance?

Bethany Wooden

It was a dark and stormy night.

That's a lousy start to my story, why can't I think of anything creative?

I sit at my desk and I look at the accusing computer screen.

"You should be writing," it says.

"I want to but I don't have time! There's never enough time," I say back to it.

But I know that's not really true. There's time, a few minutes here, a few minutes there. It's just that I'm not great at chunking down tasks and putting my focus entirely on my writing. Every time I turn around there's something else that's screaming for my attention. The family, my studies, medical appointments, the bills. Everything is desperate for its slice of my life.

I desperately want to write. The ideas burn behind my eyes. When I lie there trying to go to sleep, the ideas keep my brain whirling a million miles an hour. I can't sleep, but the instant I pick up a pen, whoosh. Ideas vanish.

In desperation I join a writer's group. Surely the answers to my problems will be there. They'll know exactly how to balance their writing and their lives.

I go along and sit in the meetings. It's glorious. Other people like me who love the art of storytelling. I'm amazed at their expertise, how varied their genres are.

I think that they will be able to fix all of my problems and finally I will get my story finished.

“Hi, I’m Amber,” I say to the gathering.

“What genre do you write in?” I’m asked. I stop, everything focuses down on that question. What genre do I write in? I’ve never thought about that question.

“Oh, a bit of this and a bit of that.” I brush off the question, because it’s difficult. I’m not great at difficult questions.

“Well, what do you like reading?” they ask. I think of everything I read, from romance to fantasy, to travel stories, to science fiction. I’m not a great fan of horror, I know that, but there are so many books that have changed my life. Where do I even start? I’m mute. I can tell that they are genuinely interested in me, but how do I put into words what is my favourite thing to read?

“Don’t worry, I like a mix of things, I can’t really decide either,” he says. Tristen, I find out, is his name. He’s about my age, with a winning smile. Bright cheerful eyes. Then there’s Sam, a retired professor, with a quirky sense of humour. We all hear about the craft of writing, then write something. I nervously read mine out and they all congratulate me on it.

What do I write?

I keep coming back to that innocent question. Amidst getting the kids ready for school, it haunts me. When I’m at my work desk, it grabs my attention. When I’m talking to my husband, there it is again.

What do I write?

I don’t know what I write, I admit to myself. Feeling ashamed, I admit defeat. I nearly give up on ever writing again, but my beautiful husband challenges me when I tell him.

"What's wrong with not knowing the answer? Can't you just muddle along for now until you find out? Isn't that part of the point of writing?" he asks. I smile and hold onto him, my sanity in a crazy world.

A month goes past and I go to another meeting. There's Tristan and Sam again, I go up to them, my hands are wringing my hem.

"How do you get the time to write?" I ask, my voice barely a whisper.

"What's that?" Sam asks me, looking at me quizzically.

"How do you get the time to write?" I say, louder this time. Sam laughs, her eyes gentle.

"I ask myself that all the time. I'm terrible about it to be honest. Although I do always try to do at least five minutes a day. It's not a lot, but it does add up over time. I also find that if I do the first five minutes, with no pressure on myself to do longer, sometimes the mood just gets me going and I look up and it's been an hour," she says.

I look at her shocked, I could never conceive of writing for a full hour. My kids would be interrupting me at least ten times in that amount of time. Sam can see it on my face. She smiles.

"The thing isn't to worry about how much time you put into writing. It's just about having fun. I'm retired. I don't have children who need my attention. My life is very different to yours. The important thing is that you find what works for you. Some people have more free time than others. That's ok."

I smile at her, grateful that she is helping me out.

It's just about having fun, huh? When was the last time I had fun writing?

I talk about it with my husband after the kids have gone to bed.

"Do you think that I could have five minutes a day to write, just time for me?" I ask. He looks incredulously into my eyes. I think that he's about to tell me I'm being selfish. I prepare to fight about it.

"Of course you can! I'm their father, I'm a parent too. I can spend time with them, we can play a boardgame or something. You love writing so much, I want you to be able to do it. That's why I told you not to give up." He has a slight frown of irritation on his brow. I get choked up, remembering why I married him. He really is on my team.

In the beginning I do just what Sam suggested. I set aside five minutes to write. The kids try to get my attention, but my husband shushes them.

"Mummy's writing. Let's play the unicorn game," he says.

"YAYYYYYY, the unicorn game," my daughter yells. Her current obsession is unicorns. Over time, the sessions stretch out, fifteen minutes seems to be my consistent result. Not only that, I'm writing more in those fifteen minutes. Slowly but surely my story comes together. I'm proud of it. I continue going to the writer's group and learning new and improved strategies and techniques for my writing. I make friends and learn so much from these other authors.

Five years pass and I'm finished editing my writing. Next step is to get it published. What do I do, where do I go? New questions consume me.

One day at the group, I hear the words I never thought I'd hear. "How do you do it? You're so good at getting your work finished?" Sally has joined the group, her life is a whirlwind of children, work and, if she's lucky, a few words into her project before she goes to sleep.

I think back to where I was before I joined the group.

I take her over to the tea and coffee table and tell her what I was told. "Just start small. Even five minutes a day adds up. Before long you will get into the flow of writing and find yourself in front of a finished first draft."

Finding my muse

Linda Visman

“My muse is a beautiful fairy queen named Titania,” a member of the group volunteers.

“Oh, mine’s a gorgeous hunk called Kurt,” chimes in another.

“I’ve heard Vera’s is a cricket who lives on her shoulder,” giggles a third. “She calls him Jiminy.”

“What’s your muse, Linda?” The leader of the writing group looks at me.

“Muse? Oh, I don’t have a muse. I just write or I don’t write. There’s no muse involved.”

“But everyone has a muse. Even the ancient Greeks had muses.”

“Well, yes. That’s where the whole thing came from. The nine daughters of Zeus and Mnemosyne. I know that Erato is the Muse of Poetry. It’s always in crossword puzzles.”

“So why don’t you have a muse?” asks the one with the hunk. “I couldn’t write without mine.”

And thus, for some writers, it goes. They have a muse. They need their muse in order to write. If their muse is having a snit or a bad hair day, they don’t help or they take off for foreign parts and take their time getting back. I’m not sure that I want a muse if they’re so pernickety. I think it’s easier to write your own words than to rely on someone who’d be so uncaring as to leave you in the lurch with no explanation.

However, I decided I had better find out more about them. Perhaps even look around and see if there was a spare one that might like to take me on for a trial period. I'd want a good solid contract though, if we clicked; no sloping off when the going gets hard. But now that I think about it, maybe I have a muse already. One that suddenly did a bunk on me last year.

I went for months unable to write more than a few scribbles. I had no inspiration, no enthusiasm, no joy in writing. Before that, I'd been on a roll, writing poetry and short stories, and really getting into my novel. Then it all stopped. Writing became a chore. I was easily distracted and couldn't focus. I was tired, and not thinking too well, but it seemed more than that. Perhaps my unknown muse had been working too hard without any acknowledgement and decided to take a break. Maybe it was suffering from burn-out. I knew I'd just have to get myself in order and my writing would pick up.

Then, a major health crisis cropped up. I expected there would be no writing going on for some months while I underwent chemotherapy. And yet, one night, lying in bed for hours unable to sleep, several brilliant ideas relating to my novel came to me. I didn't get up and write them down and when I got round to writing the next day, I couldn't remember most of them. Oh well, I was probably half dreaming anyway. Next night, I had another brilliant idea, this time for a short story. I got up and made notes. Next day, I wrote ... and wrote ... and wrote. Mmm, I wondered. What brought this on? Do I really have a muse, and has it suddenly returned from its extended holiday?

As I vacuumed the floor a couple of days later, I pondered on how and when my ideas came. I realised that, as an insomniac, it's mostly during the night that I am inspired. Lost in thought, I backed into my glass cabinet and sent several ornaments skidding across the shelves. I opened the door and rearranged the many owls I have in there, closed it and went back to the vacuum cleaner. Afterwards I returned to my study. The little silver owl that sits on my desk had fallen over, so I picked it up. Then I straightened the owl feather that's stuck on top of the monitor with Blu-Tack®.

And it hit me. If I have a muse, it must be an owl. I love owls. Their big eyes seem to hold so much knowledge and wisdom. Their feathers are so soft that they can swoop without sound. And yet they are efficient predators. They are intelligent, wise, efficient and good hunters. Are they creative too?

I've been collecting owls, usually as gifts, for about fifty years now. They come in all sizes, shapes and colours. They are made of ceramic, brass, wood, stone, glass. Some are solemn and brooding, others playful and funny. They are, in fact, very creative. So, after many years, I've decided to adopt the owl as my own muse.

I'll write every day, even when I can't think of anything to say. I'll write what is going on around me, what's in my head. I'll write a blog. Because, if I don't write I will become unable to write. It's the determination to write that makes me a writer. It's continuing to write when I've lost confidence in myself. It is writing until the words flow again and I get to that space where the real and the imagined become one inside my stories.

I'm glad I have a muse. I won't expect Owl to tell me what to write. I'll welcome him as a cherished companion, let him sit on the top of my door if he wants. I'll listen to and evaluate anything he has to tell me. But I won't clean up after him.

The need to write

Linda Visman

There's something inside me that wants to come out;
something that's churning and needs writing about.
I won't know what it is until I have penned it,
I write because nothing else seems to end it.

It's a week since last I did any writing,
and this blank page looks very inviting.
So I'll write the thoughts that I want to come out,
and then I'll discover what they're all about.

This writing's becoming addictive it seems,
I know that I'm doing it even in dreams.
It's a drug that calls to me day and night,
I must take my pen to paper and write.

It's got me so bad I write stories and verse
About wanting to write – now what could be worse?
But I've got to let out what's inside my head.
So I'll keep on writing til it's all been said.

Our living language

Jan Mitchell

Our Living Language is the name of a textbook I and my classmates used in senior high school in South Canterbury, New Zealand. The book examined the influences that led English to be the modern language we use today.

The Angles and the Saxons were two Germanic tribes that moved across from Europe to the British Isles over 2000 years ago. They displace the Celts, who were the peoples living in what is now England. The Angles first settled in the area now known as East Anglia, the Saxons nearby.

Over the years, the two groups intermingled and mixed with their neighbouring Celts. The resulting group became known as Anglo-Saxons. Meanwhile, the Celts who didn't mingle, were gradually pushed to the outlying areas of the islands. Their remnants are the Cornish, the Welsh, the Irish and the Gaelic Scots. Their languages are the remnants of the original Celtic language.

Anglo-Saxon retained some Celtic words and expressions and the resulting early language was further enriched with the Viking invasions.

We now know that many Vikings didn't just raid, plunder, then return to Scandinavia with their spoils, but many settled among the Anglo-Saxons, becoming farmers and tradespeople. The language used in those times is now called Old English.

Examples of Viking words from that time that are still in use are: street, knife, knot, knave.

The land now known as England was further invaded by the Romans early in the first century of the modern era. The Latin of the new ruling class became embedded into the vernacular. From that era, we have terminology like amorous, pedal, terminus, school.

This mixture of Anglo-Saxon and Latin is still known as Old English. It remained the language of the people of 'England' until the Norman Conquest in 1066. William the Conqueror brought French to the land, along with his nobles who became the feudal lords of the land. That mixture of French and Old English became known to language historians as Middle English.

At this time, expressions like 'aid and abet' became common. Aid is from the verb aider in French via Latin and abet is from Middle English.

As usually happens, the invading conquerors became assimilated into the population. Middle English, a mixture of Anglo-Saxon, Latin and French, became the language of the upper classes and the older dialects remained the language of the poorer people.

By the time of Elizabeth I, England was looking outward to the rest of the world. The monarch sent out explorers like Sir Francis Drake to search for riches to help pay for England's wars against the French and Spanish. As these pirates with a warrant from the Queen plundered foreign ships and far distant lands, notions of colonisation grew.

The British Empire was probably at its height under the reign of Queen Victoria, who became the Empress of India as well as the Queen of the colonies of Canada and other parts of North America, of South Africa, Rhodesia, Kenya, Tanganyika, Nigeria, Burma, Malaya, Australia, New Zealand, the Falkland Islands, South Georgia and perhaps some other places I have forgotten. Most of these nations became The Commonwealth of Britain after WWII, when Britain could no longer afford to maintain her position of overlord.

As ever, the conqueror became assimilated to a degree in the lands she ruled and so parts of those languages became part of modern English. Thus, we have humpy and bushranger (Australia), bach and crib (New Zealand), Nabob (India), veldt (South Africa), cookie and hamburger (America), kris (Malay) and many more.

It is strange therefore, that as well as being taught that English is a living and growing language, unlike Latin, which is dead, 'proper' English was also instilled into us in high school. Only uneducated people ever said 'them things', 'youse' and 'we was'. Now, these expressions are recognised as part of the creole language of Aboriginal Australians.

As a result of the distinction between proper English and a growing, living language, I find myself in a bind. I loved the introduction of the word 'hassle' in the late 1960s, because there was no word in English to express that exact meaning. Yet, I shudder every time I hear a person say, 'I had a lay down'. I used to tell my students at Cheltenham G.H.S. that 'people lie and hens lay'. I blame the Americans for the wrong usage of lie and lay. They have mixed them up for far longer than Australians. Unless you were taught extensive grammar in school, you wouldn't know that while there is a verb 'to lay', 'lay' is also the past tense of the verb 'to lie'. No wonder it is confusing.

Unless they have learned a foreign language, even middle-aged people today do not know how to decline a verb. I wonder how many of you reading this even know what I mean by that expression, 'to decline'? A declension is the setting out of all the parts and tenses of a verb.

I also detest the relatively new usage of the past participle of verbs containing a ‘u’ (eg. sung) being used instead of the simple past tense, ‘sang’. Thus we have I sing, I sang, I have sung; you sink, you sank, you have sunk; he swims, he swam, he has swum. Instead, someone might announce that ‘Ian Thorpe swum his final race’ and that ‘the boat sunk’.

Now that the ABC announcers are using these past participles for the simple past tense, maybe I should shrug and tell myself that English is a living language and, as such, will develop, change and grow according to people’s usage.

Section 2

How we write

From habits to hints, inspiration to revision, this section offers a glimpse into our writing processes. Each of us works differently, but together we share the tools and techniques that help us shape stories worth telling.

Memoir moments: why write memoir

Linda Visman

I wrote this item for MacMuse as an exercise to get members to think about writing their own memories.

What is History?

Once upon a time history was seen as about important people in the past; kings or inventors who made something happen that affected local, national or international events. Many people still tend to look at history that way, but that is far from the truth. Historians now look almost as much to the present as to the past to see how and why events occur as they do.

They also look at things from a micro as well as macro perspective, to ordinary individuals doing ordinary things, instead of looking only at major political, economic and social systems. You can see this in the huge increase over the last thirty or forty years or so in local history studies, and in the growth of family history and memoir writing.

Why Write Memoir?

We write memoir for several different reasons. Instead of life continuing at a relatively steady rate, with little change over decades or even centuries, where each generation faced the same way of life as their parents and their grandparents, the rapid changes in technology, in travel and in communications, each generation now faces a different world to the last.

Following on from this, some write memoir in order to pass on to their family, where they came from, what life was like for them and how things have changed since they were young. An increasingly common reason is to make sense of their life, or aspects of it in order to come to understand relationships, or to come to terms with trauma.

A Memoir Exercise

I love to write about little things that happened to me in the past, or about what it was like to live in a post WWII society. Perhaps you do that too, or would you like to tell some of your stories to your grandchildren but haven't gotten around to it yet? Well, now is your chance to start putting them down. I intend to add a memoir writing exercise to each issue of *MacMuse*. For those who already write memoir, here is a chance to focus on the smaller things in your past. I will start with something most of you will remember with pleasure.

Your Childhood Television Experience

How old were you when your family first got a television? If you are younger, when did you first get a colour TV? For those who grew up with TV in black and white, or in colour, what were your favourite programs? Did you love Playschool as a child? Did you prefer westerns over comedy? What about drama series, music and dance programs?

Choose one thing from your childhood TV watching experience and write about it. You don't have to write much, but bring out the feeling of the time, the experience, and the pleasure (or otherwise) and share it with us.

How successful authors learn to write better – insights from LMFAW

Steve Shipley

We all learn in different ways, some approaches being far more effective than others, depending on how we absorb and retain information. Whether it's through reading books, watching videos, taking courses, taking part in writing clubs, or simply writing more, the most crucial part of any author's journey is a commitment to ongoing learning and improvement. This article highlights insights gathered from a survey of the Lake Macquarie Fellowship of Australian Writers (LMFAW) members, revealing the top ways they sharpen their craft and the books they recommend.

A Diverse Approach to Learning

When surveyed, LMFAW members shared various ways they develop their writing skills.

Here's a breakdown of their top learning activities:

- Reading books on writing (67%): For many authors, studying the craft directly through books remains essential.
- Joining writing groups (67%): Engaging in supportive communities helps authors exchange feedback and stay motivated.
- Writing more (58%): Consistent practice is vital. Each project, whether a short story or novel, adds to their skills and experience.

- Peer critiques (58%): Authors value constructive feedback as it provides an objective view of their strengths and areas for improvement.
- Reading blogs and articles (50%): Supplementing formal resources, blogs and articles offer quick insights and keep authors up to date with industry trends.
- As a group, authors find value in reading more, writing more, and sharing their work with others to stand out in a competitive field.

> ***Despite advancements in technology and the evolving landscape of publishing, the timeless essence of storytelling and writing persists.***

The Books That Made the Biggest Impact

We asked the LMFAW membership to share the books that shaped their approach to writing. Here are the standout recommendations, organised by the value each book brought to the members.

Gold Award Winner

On Writing by Stephen King (2000)

This was the top 'must-read' for over half of the members. King's blend of memoir and writing advice provides insight into the life and work habits of a prolific author. It covers the basics of grammar, style, and storytelling with inspirational wisdom. *On Writing* is ideal for those who want a relatable, down-to-earth guide on how to become a writer and live the writer's life.

Silver Award Winner

Story Engineering by Larry Brooks (2011)

Larry Brooks offers a systematic approach to storytelling that resonates well with those who prefer structure in their writing. This book covers the key elements of storytelling, from plot to character arcs, making it a favourite for writers who like detailed guidance on crafting a story.

Four Bronze Award Winners (tie)

Structuring Your Novel by K.M. Weiland (2013)

Like Brooks, Weiland emphasises the importance of structure but breaks down the process in a way that's accessible even to new writers. Her step-by-step approach has helped numerous authors understand how to outline and frame their novels effectively.

Save the Cat by Blake Snyder (2005)

Originally written for screenwriters, Snyder's book has become a classic among fiction writers, too. It provides a template for creating engaging stories with a focus on pacing and character development, offering practical advice that can apply to novels as much as scripts.

Writing Your Life Story by Graham L. Ascough (2006)

For those interested in memoirs or personal storytelling, Ascough's book is a guiding light. It covers not only the mechanics of writing, but also the emotional aspect of sharing personal stories with authenticity.

Elements of Style by Strunk and White (originally published 1918)

This timeless classic is a go-to for authors who want clarity and conciseness. Though short, it's packed with essential principles that form the backbone of good writing. From punctuation rules to tips on improving style, Strunk and White's guide remains as relevant today as when it was first published.

Reading and Writing Regularly Are Key

Beyond the books and resources, a recurring theme emerged: read widely within your genre. This helps members understand their readers' expectations and discover unique approaches that can make their work stand out.

Though the list above captures some of the most impactful books, there are countless other resources out there for those looking to expand their author library. This curated selection by the LMFAW is a great starting point for anyone seeking reliable and effective writing guides.

Happy Reading and Happy Writing!

Writing is a journey, and there's no 'one-size-fits-all' formula for success. Find the resources that resonate with you, stay connected with other writers, and continue to hone your craft. As you do, you'll not only grow as a writer but also cultivate a unique voice that stands out to readers.

Make your life a story, not a report

Linda Visman

Who wants to hear that you did this, and then you did that or went here or there, events recited one after another as if it were a police witness statement? Nobody does; not even your most loving friends and family.

Remember that your life is not a continuous narrative that goes from birth to death. Unless you have a fantastic memory and perfect recall, you cannot tell the full story anyway. And is your story important enough that people would want a blow-by-blow of your life?

What you really need to do is distil the essence of certain aspects of your life - the things you think are important that illustrate those aspects. But again, caution! You always need to remember that when you tell of incidents and talk about people, you are presenting an interpretation of them - your interpretation.

It is your interpretation that you should go with, but you also need, as much as possible, to take into account the interpretation of others who were there. They will have their own story from their perspective and may be able to enhance your memory of it.

Thinking about the aspects of your life you want to focus on can be rather daunting. For example, should you follow major themes? Do you know what is or isn't relevant to these themes? How do you tackle such a major project?

All these questions can be tackled by taking one approach, at least for a start. So that you don't feel overwhelmed, begin recording your story with one memory, no matter how small, but it should be something important to you. Write it and think about it. Then re-write it so that you have the ***essence of the memory*** that story. You may write only a few hundred words or less. Then tackle another small memory, then another.

As you write these memories, you will probably find that some of the stories are connected in some way. You may see that certain themes have emerged. Say you have two or three themes emerging. Go back to your short pieces and see which ones fit into which theme; some may fit more than one. Then, if you haven't already found yourself doing so, recall any other relevant memories that fit the theme. Choose one theme. If one of these themes you have thought/written about stands out as being something that shaped your life, you should probably focus on that.

Thus, as you write your memories, you are doing three things at once: developing themes; finding what is relevant; and tackling a major project a small bite at a time.

Finally, if you want to keep the interest of a reader, then you must make a story. You must make it immediate and interesting, bringing your readers along with you. One way to create immediacy is to write as if you are writing fiction. Use the tools of fiction to bring in all the things that make a scene or story glow – characterisation, setting and dialogue, emotion, and immediacy, and use the five senses to create a sense of being there.

So, if you have a story you want to tell, go for it.

Collaborative writing, some personal observations

Pam Garfoot

I really enjoyed the general meeting we held on Saturday 17 October 2020 as the topic was one that really resonated with me – **collaborative writing.** I am currently working on my second collaboratively written book and have a few insights that I hope are useful to members.

My first co-written book, a family history called *Making them real,* was published in 2012. My sister (Elizabeth Conway) and I wrote the book together without the benefit of today's collaborative tools – tools which would have made the task so much easier.

Initially we worked together to decide a basic structure and outline, and to roughly allocate chapters and tasks according to our interests and skills. So far, so good. After this we each wrote portions of the book using word processing software (my sister using Word and me using Open Office software – our first big challenge).

Over a period of many months we suggested changes and flicked the documents back and forth in mark-up format between us to resolve the different approaches and writing styles that we had. This worked well enough, up to a point. Open Office and Word handled mark-up changes differently, so that was one issue. Version control was another massive challenge.

One of our worst disasters came when we lost track of who had the 'master' version of one of the book's sections, and both ended up making many suggestions (and accepting and rejecting previous suggestions) in different versions of the same document. What a mess! We sorted this out and then developed a rather cumbersome but effective system of ensuring that such a catastrophe didn't happen again.

Ultimately our book was completed and published 2012, and it was, in time, awarded the Queensland Family History Society's Book Award for 2014.

Ever suckers for punishment, in about 2017 we again began to collaborate on another book, this time on an event in Queensland pioneer history that was tangential to our family history.

Capricorn drover, the story of an epic droving journey right across the colony of Queensland in 1878, is now nearing its final draft. Our decision to make use of Google Drive, as our collaboration tool, has made the task a comparative breeze. We have not only been able to store and share our research materials using Google Drive, but have also done all of our writing using Google Docs.

Having undertaken two substantial collaborative projects, I have been able to distil a few 'learnings' which might be useful to others contemplating a similar project, whether it is a non-fiction work or a piece of fictional writing.

Firstly, you need to **trust** the person you are working with. An approach to sharing and collaborating needs to be established and you both need to stick to it.

Compromise is key to success. No matter how closely your writing styles seem to be aligned there will be differences in approach. Your collaborator may want, for instance, to change or even delete a piece of your writing you are attached to. You need to be able to put your ego aside and understand your collaborator's point of view.

Of course, compromise means that you need to '**pick your battles**'. You may need to go along with a particular suggestion because you want to stand your ground over something else.

On the plus side, having a collaborator is rather like having an editor and proofreader on tap. Your collaborator will see errors that have passed you by, and you will be able to offer useful insights on their writing too.

Successful collaborations can be a lot of fun. It's great to be able to share a writing journey with someone else. And it can produce some really strong and polished writing. After all Stephen King, Terry Pratchett and Candice Fox have all done it.

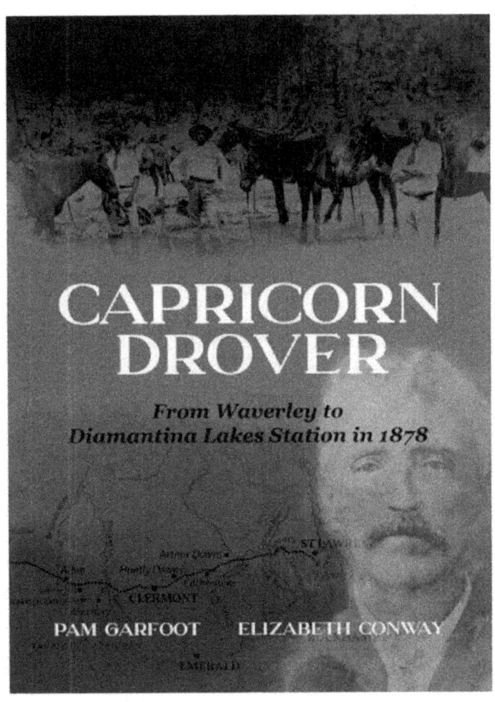

Article written 2020.
Capricorn Drover *was published in 2023*

English is a pretty weird language

Pam Garfoot

Yes, English certainly *is* a weird language. This weirdness comes courtesy of the many influences (Latin, Greek, French, Indian and many more) that have contributed words, pronunciations and forms of expression to it. So, let me count some of the ways that English is plain peculiar:

- Why are all these words pronounced differently?
  cough, rough, though, bough, through
- Why is it that writers write and painters paint, but fingers don't fing? Why don't grocers groce, why don't hammers ham, and why don't hipsters hipst?
- If the past tense form of complete is completed, then why wouldn't the past tense of go be goed?

- Why does it sound right to say “that nice little old plump spotty dog” but not to say “that old spotty plump little nice dog”?
- Why do some words (like clip, refrain, cleave, transparent) have multiple meanings some of which are the complete opposite of each other?
- If i goes before e, except after c, and except as in ‘neighbour’ and ‘weigh’ then why are there words like weird, heist, leisure, neither and surfeit?
- Weird: i before e except when your foreign neighbour Keith receives eight counterfeit beige sleighs from feisty caffeinated weightlifters.
- Why do so many words not sound like they look? Think: queue, debt, island, doubt, receipt

The list goes on. With all this weirdness to contend with, it’s a wonder we ever become accomplished writers. But somehow, with work, we do.

Picnic table

Linda Visman

I thought it was a friendly chat at first – an elderly couple at a picnic table by the lake enjoying the winter sun and each other's company.

Then their posture changed. He sat with his back against the table, she at the edge of the bench seat, facing away from him, elbows on knees, back and head bowed.

As I walked closer, I heard an angry voice. His. Gesturing hand, stiff posture. He sounded as though he was justifying himself. If she replied, I didn't hear it. He raised a beer can to his lips. She held one between her drooping hands. I hadn't noticed the cans before.

In no mood to listen to someone else's anger and its futility, I turned and walked the other way.

When I glanced over again later, her posture was the same as it had been previously, but he had turned away from her completely, arms and legs crossed, body tense.

I wouldn't like to have gone home with them when they left. I wondered what imagined bond, kept them together.

Do you take note of other people's attitudes, bearing, voice, actions, etc when you are out? What great material for writing real people!

Dictionaries aren't all the same

John Franks

The *Oxford English Dictionary* was to be based on actual evidence of words in use, taken from printed sources dating from all periods of the language's history from medieval times to the present. The first part (or fascicle, to use the technical term) was issued in 1884. Finally, in April 1928, the last part was published to critical acclaim. The final work consisted of ten volumes containing over 250,000 main entries. The second edition of the OED, published in 1989 filled 22,000 pages bound into twenty substantial volumes. It had 273,000 headwords; 171,476 of them being in current use, 47,156 being obsolete words and around 9,500 derivative words included as subentries.

The Dictionary of Lost Words is the debut novel by Australian author Pip Williams, published in March 2020. It became a best-seller in Australia and was also a New York Times best-seller. It weaves together themes of language, feminism, social change, and the importance of preserving marginalised voices.

The Urban Dictionary was intended as a dictionary of slang or cultural words and phrases, not typically found in standard English dictionaries, but it is now used to define any word, event, or phrase (including sexually explicit content).

Grammar: then and now, *or* Why can't the English learn to speak/write?

John Franks and Pam Garfoot

We live in a changing world. Language and grammar changes have been happening for centuries. For example, the grammar, spelling and pronunciation in Chaucer's *The Canterbury tales* and that in Shakespeare's works both have words and expressions we struggle to comprehend today. In fact, many modern writers struggle to cope with the grammar, spelling and syntax that only thirty or so years ago were second nature to us.

Let's look at some basics about language. The major native dialects of English may be divided by linguists into regional categories including the British Isles, North America, Australasia, Africa, India, the Caribbean and a growing list of others. They can be associated not only with place but also with particular social groups.

Within a given English-speaking country, there is generally a form of the language considered to be Standard English. We see it reflected in dictionaries like the *Oxford English Dictionary* (OED) which set the standard for spoken and written English for generations. The OED started in 1857, when a proposal was put before the Philological Society in London identifying deficiencies and inconsistencies in the English language. Many of these dated back to Dr Johnson's influential but faulty dictionary of 1755.

The proposal called for a complete re-examination of the English language from the Old English of Anglo-Saxon times, through the Middle English of the Norman Conquest in 1066, to Modern English which emerged in the sixteenth century and continues to the present.

The first *Oxford English Dictionary* took an astonishing seventy years to complete. The latest update to the OED includes almost 700 new and revised words and phrases, including *babyccino*, *freecycling* and *jillionaire*. A relatively recent addition to the OED is the word *woke* (an Old English past tense or past participle of wake) added to the OED as late as 2017. *Woke* now encompasses a meaning relating to alertness to racial prejudice, discrimination and social injustices, sexism, and denial of LGBTQI rights. Such is the complexity of our language in the present day.

So how do we come to terms with these complexities? One might presume it is through learning informally at home from infancy then learning formal grammar rules at school. A writer must, to a reasonable extent, meet the challenge of Standard English to make a work accessible to readers. In doing so there are conventional rules of which a writer must be aware. However, in modern writing, an author should identify his or her readership and also fit grammar and word choices to the culture of his or her characters. Writers do not always need to adhere to the rules of grammar but as a rule of thumb, one needs to know the rules before one breaks them.

One can easily see that learning to write English to achieve the communication of ideas at an effective level can be a daunting task. Clear concise English allows the reader to focus on the purpose of writing: communication with one's readership.

Many prescriptive textbooks of the 18th, 19th and 20th centuries informed us of good, non-ambiguous grammatical English construction and usage. However, they didn't always achieve their purpose. Most of them were based on the Latin constructions of declining nouns and conjugating verbs.

There are nine parts of speech in the English language: Noun, Pronoun, Verb, Adjective, Adverb, Preposition, Conjunction, Article and Interjection or Exclamation. The part of speech indicates how the word functions in meaning, as well as grammatically, within the sentence. All the parts of speech perform specified duties in written English and, when writing, you may not want your readers to have to stop and decipher your work.

To add to the complexity of English, thousands of words, with their variety of spellings, have been borrowed from other languages over many centuries. In modern times the vocabulary of English has been consciously enhanced to meet an increasing variety of purposes, including the description of new scientific and technology activities, greater awareness of dialects and slang terminology.

English is a global language or lingua franca. There are English speakers in most countries, the language having been carried there by colonial, imperial and commercial activity, the slave trade, and recently, economic, cultural and educational demands. English encounters demands that blur the grammatical lines between standard and non-standard English.

The conventions in writing are extensive. However, they may be broken depending on context. Context refers to the circumstances surrounding a text that shape its meaning. Raymond Chandler, an American-British novelist and screenwriter, had a distinctive style that frequently challenged conventional grammar rules.

The story goes that on one occasion he submitted a script to his editor in which he had split an infinitive verb. *To shoot* is an infinitive verb, and *to cold-bloodedly shoot* is an example of a split infinitive. The editor corrected the manuscript and sent it back to Chandler. His response was "When I split an infinitive, I want it to stay split".

Chandler was a master of storytelling but also had a distinctive style that challenged conventional grammar rules in favour of clarity, rhythm, and style over strict adherence to traditional grammar norms. His approach to writing included his willingness to bend the rules for the sake of effective communication. Nevertheless, to effectively break rules as writers we must first know the rules which we wish to break.

It seems that learning grammar is no longer a priority in crowded school curriculums. It is being outsourced to hopefully reliable textbook producers, television and social media, and frequently not valued at all. Those of us who learnt grammar many years ago often find we have lost touch with its finer points. Often tools embedded in the software we use (spell checkers, grammar checkers and the like) are not sufficient to ensure flawless grammar.

Consequently, our group's critique sessions often need to cover some basic aspects of grammar, syntax and punctuation. Some of the areas our group of writers has most difficulty with include tense, point-of-view, punctuation, sentence structure and run-on sentences, modern spellings, syntax and more. Grammar is just one of the many things we must try to master to make progress in becoming better writers.

So, what is grammar?

It is a set of rules for organising written and spoken language. Principal elements of grammar include an understanding of:

- ***Syntax*** *(word order in a sentence, such as subject / verb / action. For example, Jane went swimming)*
- ***Parts of speech*** *(nouns, pronouns, verbs, adjectives, adverbs, prepositions, conjunctions, articles, interjections). Without an understanding of how these are used correctly, a reader or listener may misunderstand the meaning of any text*
- ***Punctuation*** *(a set of symbols used in writing to divide words and clauses and to show how the sentence should be read and understood)*
- ***Spelling*** *(the forming of words from letters according to accepted usage of written language, a significant contributor to clarity and understanding).*

Inspiration

Linda Visman

I wonder whence ideas come?
Not always when expected –
Sometimes when you're feeling great, and
Particularly connected.
I've also found, at certain times,
Rational thought is not important;
Amazingly ideas come
To minds that seem quite mordant!
In point of fact it's oft asserted, and
Observation does support it, that
Nine out of ten ideas come – when sitting on the toilet!

Reading: how it helps us as writers

Pam Garfoot and Sandra Boyd

Stephen King says that "if you want to be a writer, you must do two things above all others: read a lot and write a lot."

We explored the topic of reading at a 2024 meeting. Firstly, we explored some of the ways reading helps us to improve as writers. These include:

- Exposing us to different writing styles and genres
- Helping us to subconsciously absorb syntax, grammar, style and punctuation in context - and helping us to see how these rules may be skilfully broken at times (syntax being the arrangement of words and phrases in a specific order)
- Helping us to subconsciously absorb generic conventions, writing structure, and document design
- Giving us increased insight and inspiration
- Helping us to develop critical thinking skills
- Helping us to expand our vocabularies and teaching us how to play with language
- Improving concentration and helping remove writer's block
- Improving memory and cognitive function (reading has been described as 'jogging for the brain')
- Expanding our knowledge of the world
- Bringing discipline to our lives
- Improving our knowledge of trends in writing, and what readers love to read about
- Helping us to further develop our own 'writer's voice'.

Next, we discussed some of the good books each of us had read recently and tried to analyse what it was about them that made them good. Here are some of our favourites of the moment:

- Bronwyn *The Riders* by Tim Winton (1994)
- Linda *Amber and Alice* by Janette Paul (2017)
- Kristen *Harrow the Ninth* by Tamsyn Muir (2021)
- Alison *Emergency Skin* by N K Jemisin (2019)
- Joan *Ten Audacious Women* by Margaret McKay & Susan Rose Baker (2021)
- George *The Mathematics of Secrets* by Joshua Holden (2018)
- Sandra *The Dictionary of Lost Words* by Pip Williams (2020)
- Bethany *Kingdom of Ash* by Sarah J Maas (2023)
- John *A Gentleman in Moscow* by Amor Towles (2018)
- Cate *Tales from Shakespeare* by Charles and Mary Lamb (1807)
- Rob *Queen of Sorcery* by David Eddings (2012)
- Pam *The Others* by Mark Brandi (2021)
- Steve *The ONE Thing* by Gary Keller (2014);
- Steve *The Successful Author Mindset* by Joanna Penn (2016)

Section 3

How the group functions

A writers' group doesn't last twenty-five years by accident. Here, we share some of the practical and personal ingredients – structure, support, skills, trust, and humour – that have kept us showing up, growing together, and writing better, year after year.

Finance: incomings and outgoings

George Graves

I think most of the members of our group would prefer to watch drab grey paint dry than to look at a page with lots of numbers on it. So, I will attempt to minimise the number of numbers.

In a group like ours that meets, at times, in a rented room, or has invited speakers who have come to discuss some interesting topic about writing or to tell us about their latest book and how they have come to write it, we really do need someone to pay the bills and to bank the money. Someone to look after the finances. A treasurer.

So, this note is about *the money*.

What money do we collect and where does it all go? Over the years has this changed?

When we rent a room, such as one at the Toronto Multi-Purpose Centre (TMPC) or the Hub, or a room at the Toronto Library, we each make a small contribution to its hiring cost. The treasurer then deposits the money in The Greater bank account. I have only been in the group for a little over ten years and we have always done that.

At times, the amount collected for the room-hire does not cover its cost. Money from our bank account then pays the difference.

As we are members of the Lake Macquarie FAW, we are members of the Fellowship of Australian Writers NSW. Of the membership money we collect each year, due in December, we send most of it to FAW(NSW). In return, they send a magazine, *Writers Voice*, to each of us. Our insurance is also covered by them. This is important for those times when we meet in homes.

When the group was first formed, the membership fees were $25 per year. In January 2013, the fees were increased to $45 as the State (FAW(NSW)) had increased their fees to $40. (The branch retained $5 for its own needs). Our fees are now $50. For a span of twenty-five years, I think that a change from $25 to $50 is a fairly small increase.

We retain a little of the money which is used for costs associated with afternoon teas, printing and a host of other small items.

Every two years, we run a writing competition from within our group. We were due to have one in 2024 but it was postponed until 2025 to coincide with the 25th anniversary of the formation of our branch. The Alice Sinclair Memorial Writing Competition is named after Alice Sinclair who joined the group shortly after it was formed and was one of the early presidents. The first few of these competitions barely broke even: the total entry fees were about the same as the value of the prizes. However, for the latest two, we received many entries from all over Australia and, after the presentation of the prizes and the honorarium to those who were the judges, there was some profit.

Of course, we run the writing competition only for fun and to promote excellence in writing. However, the profits were appreciated as they made our funding more secure.

We have published two anthologies. The first one, *Beneath the Surface*, contained short stories and poems from writers within our group. It was very well received and the sale of the books was more than the cost of publishing. The second one, *Out of the Shadows*, with the top fifteen short stories and fifteen poems from one of our writing competitions, did not sell so well and there was a deficit.

So, what has changed over the years?

We have more visiting speakers now than, say, ten years ago. About three a year now and I think this is wonderful. We can learn to appreciate many different styles of writing, short stories, different genres of books, and poems. Of course, we give the speakers a small amount of money as an appreciation for their time, effort and cost of coming to present to our group. (At other times, members of our group lead the discussion. They come free!)

One thing that we have not spent money on, for many years now, has been an "outing". I can remember the trips to The Old Brush, where we sat under the trees, looked at the kangaroos, and wrote about what inspired us.

One time we visited a shop that sold lots of delicious chocolates. Only chocolates. Oh, the aroma! (And the taste, for those people who enjoy chocolate). It may have been on the way to The Old Brush. Although people paid for their entry into The Old Brush, or for their chocolates, there were always some small amounts picked up by group finances. Life seems even busier now than then. If we were to run an excursion now, perhaps few people would come.

Overall, our group has more people in it now than many years ago. The initial number was high, at over thirty members. The number fluctuates and I only mention this as the number of members affects our finances. However, it is not the actual number that matters – it is the enthusiasm of the people within the group that is important – their keenness to write, to read and to encourage others.

In the early days, the group did not have much in the way of savings. There are various bank balances, such as $260, $624, $498, $689 and $417 recorded in the early committee minutes. The need for fundraising was also recorded several times. The amount grew to $1,752 in March 2011.

Our finances are in a healthier state than about ten years ago. When I volunteered to become treasurer, we had slightly more than one thousand dollars in the bank. Unfortunately, after three years, the amount slowly decreased each year. We decided we needed to increase the yearly membership fee from $45 to $50 to arrest the decline. (That is for full membership. Students have always been half price.) We have kept that amount the same for many years now.

The writing competitions, anthologies and some donations have increased the amount in the bank. We can publish an anthology now, costing about $2,000, without being concerned that we may not have enough money for the payments before the sales give us some income. (In the past, people have offered to put the cost on their card if we felt it was the only way we could publish the first anthology. Fortunately, that wonderful offer was not needed).

As well as The Greater bank account, we have a petty cash account. We use this for reimbursing people for small items such as cards for speakers, stamps, printing, afternoon tea supplies and other miscellaneous debits. A file is kept of the receipts. Nothing much has changed about the small amount kept in this account. It is looked after by the treasurer.

Overall, I think our finances are now in quite a good state. It has been fun, and at times something of a challenge, being a treasurer for the group.

MacMuse, the newsletter of the Lake Macquarie Fellowship of Australian Writers

Linda Visman

The first official meeting of the newly formed writing group was held in September 2000. The topic of producing a newsletter arose, as a source of regular news about meetings, activities, and information on writing topics, and for members to share their writing. Because the group was centred on Lake Macquarie, this newsletter became *The Macquarie Muse.*

The first issue of four pages was produced in November 2000. It contained summaries of the discussion topics at the September and October meetings: "The Joy of Writing" and "Giving and Receiving Feedback". The editorial committee was led by the president, Anna Scott. The second and third issues, by then eight pages, went out in April and September of 2001. Macquarie Muse received the FAW's regional newsletter award in 2001.

After that the newsletter became quarterly. In 2004, the content was still put together by the committee, but Keith Davey became its producer, setting it out and having it printed.

Over the years, the newsletter adapted as each new editor/producer brought their own style to its presentation. In 2006, *Macquarie Muse* became *MacMuse*. Content expanded to cover a variety of topics: members' own creative endeavours like short stories and poetry, and also articles on how to improve writing mostly contributed by the members, details of writing competitions, reports on guest speakers and writing events, book and movie reviews and more.

In 2008, under the editor/producer Linda Stewart, *MacMuse* gradually changed from print to digital as more and more members embraced the use of email. Within three years it was fully electronic.

Autumn 2008

MacMuse

Inside this issue:

The Sydney Writers' Festival is just around the corner once more, and perhaps it is a good time to reflect on the whole purpose of writing – why we do it in the first place. It can be humbling to sit with great writers and listen to their processes. In my experience of these events, the ways in which they arrive at the end product are almost as varied as the multitude of authors. What they seem to have in common is a passion for self expression.

A friend recently asked me why all of these writing groups exist. Do the members all hope to be published? . It was an interesting question that had me thinking about motivation. Do we all expect to have our work published? If so, how do we cope with the knowledge that, statistically, not one in ten thousand will achieve this holy grail? I believe the answer lies elsewhere. Could the existence of writing groups be as simple as being involved in a process that is both expressive and creative for its own sake?

As this will be my last report, I would like to let you all in on a secret. You have an executive committee that is second to none. It has been a privilege to be nurtured by them as we have worked through the issues of the day. Their hard work and humour have made it a pleasure to be in their company.

Linda (V) is a Secretary extraordinaire. Whilst writing three novels, short stories and poetry, she still finds time to keep us all functioning. The editorial group compiling Macmuse, Rina and Jo, have a passion for the written word that encourages us all to try harder. To both the members of the committee and the members at large, I say thank you for your enthusiasm and support. You have a great organisation in which I believe you can be justly proud.

Whilst I relinquish the role of President, I will continue as a member of this group.

Thankyou.

Terry.

In July 2009, Linda Visman succeeded Linda Stewart as editor/producer, adding new sections for member achievements, a poetry page, a section for memoir writing, a last-page emoji that shared humorous ideas and quotations, and reviving the editor's challenge from early issues. The challenge only lasted about a year as not enough members responded.

In 2008/09, Linda Stewart's *MacMuse* won NSW FAW's best branch newsletter award. In 2013/14, *MacMuse* again took out the award under editor/producer Linda Visman.

As a newsletter distributed only to LMFAW members and for sharing only within the group, any original writing *MacMuse* contains is not considered to be published, and thus can be submitted to competitions and publishers elsewhere. It has been a wonderful way for members to see, perhaps for the first time, their work in print.

Just as LMFAW grew from a small group of enthusiastic writers seeking fellowship in their local area to what may be the largest and most convivial FAW group in NSW, so also has *MacMuse* grown. What began as a few shared pages twice a year is now a document of twenty or more pages, keeping members informed and sharing their writing, in-house. Linda Visman, who had put out her first issue of *MacMuse* as editor, number 37, in July 2010, produced issue number 100 in July 2022. In December of that year, Linda passed the *MacMuse* editor/ producer mantle into the capable hands and creative mind of Bronwyn MacRitchie.

The growth and strength of *MacMuse* is thanks to all the members who, over the years, have shared their creative writing, knowledge and advice with others in our branch. *MacMuse* would not exist, or at least would not be so successful, without that membership support.

New ways: the impact of the COVID-19 pandemic for our group

Pam Garfoot

There would be very few people living in Australia whose lives were not significantly affected by the COVID pandemic of 2020. There were major impacts for members of the Lake Macquarie FAW too – not all of them bad.

We began our year routinely enough with a February general meeting which focused on how we would be approaching the long-awaited production of our group's first anthology (eventually published as *Beneath the Surface*). However, there was uneasiness in the air, the first reported case of COVID in Australia having occurred back in January.

In March we hosted a workshop presented by one of our favourite guest speakers, Jaye Ford. Jaye's workshop proved to be the last in-person one we held for the rest of the year. By the end of the month, deaths from COVID were occurring in Australia and lockdown was upon us.

None of us met up in April, and the Committee was at a temporary loss as to how we could keep going as a group. We were, after all, a community of writers so 'coming together' was our thing. However, after some initial uncertainty, we re-focused and decided that, having accepted membership fees, we needed to offer something of value to our members. If ever there was a need to support members this was the time to do it – but how? Technologies which were largely new to us proved to be the solution.

The first area we focused on was critiquing. Many members used the enforced lockdown periods to actually write and they sought feedback on what they had written. We continued to offer critique but Google Drive (a shared space in the 'cloud') had to be our collaboration zone. From May our normal schedule of critique sessions was maintained and pieces were uploaded to Google Drive for online critique. With the new way of doing things our learning curve was steep.

Quite a number of members did not wish to use Google Drive (for various reasons) and, consequently, we did continue email communications. Guidelines and support for using Google Drive were offered to those who needed it. Soon critique using our new collaboration space became a fairly routine (and largely successful) activity for us.

From our May 2020 general meeting date onwards we gathered around our computer screens for Zoom sessions. Again, there was a steep learning curve for many of us and all the usual obstacles: the need for a paid subscription to allow meetings longer than 40 minutes, connectivity problems, issues with camera and audio, and learning a different sort of meeting etiquette.

Our meeting topics included developing confidence in writing, writing limericks, working collaboratively, and several writing exercises. In November we even announced the outcome of the Alice Sinclair Memorial Writing Competition at our Zoom meeting and invited winners to join us.

It was surprising to us that, over the year, our membership numbers actually grew. In retrospect it seems that people really value creative (and other) community groups when times are tough.

By March 2021, a year after we had last properly met, our in-person general meetings began again. Another round of lockdown in the latter half of the year saw us return, fairly seamlessly, to Zoom meetings for a while. We were 'old hands' by then. By December (fortunately a quiet period for us) our region became a huge hot-spot for COVID infections.

2022 saw us re-establish our in-person meetings, which are certainly our preferred way of operating. Despite this, in the years since COVID, we have continued to use the technologies we introduced to the group in lockdown times.

We continue to upload critique pieces to Google Drive to allow input by those members who cannot physically get to meetings. We have also widened considerably the scope of our use of Google Drive, now having two main spaces – one for the general membership where critique submissions, newsletters, photos and a wide variety of things are available, and one for the use of the Committee only. Additionally, one critique session each month is now held via Zoom. Other meetings are occasionally held via Zoom too.

In short, we have experienced quite a revolution, mostly beneficial, in the way our group meets and collaborates.

LMFAW: a State Committee perspective

Cate Plink

Before I begin to talk about LMFAW I would like to refresh everybody's memory on exactly what the Aims of the Fellowship of the Australian Writers are.

1. To foster and endorse the growth of Australian writing.
2. To promote excellence in writing.
3. To encourage writers and those interested in writing to join the Fellowship and enjoy the support, help and knowledge of members.
4. To expand the Fellowship across the State.
5. To provide an organisation to assist writers unable to attend Branch meetings.
6. To take the Fellowship into the 21st century and take advantage of technology and its new role in writing and publishing.

When I joined LMFAW in 2016 it was the first time I'd joined a new branch since I had become Vice President of the State Committee. I found that I was looking at the branch from a new perspective. The aims of the organisation had been the subject of much discussion during my time on the committee.

The updated and revised ones had been adopted fairly recently, and it became obvious that they are divided between the branch and the state, so I would like to look at how LMFAW follows through as a branch.

1. Although the onus for this may be thought to be a state responsibility, it is actually a branch one, and this branch took it seriously.

2. Some of the branches I have attended have monthly homework which each member reads out during the meeting. I found this interesting and helpful, and it did help my own writing somewhat. Some also run workshops separately from the meetings where different aspects of writing are covered. Again, they were very helpful. With LMFAW however there are workshops every meeting. Some with outside presenters, and some run by members with different areas of expertise to share. Everybody is encouraged to write a short piece at the end of the session, and it has been interesting to watch new writers blossom as they learn different writing skills and techniques. The critique meetings that are held each month separately to the general meetings are enormously helpful to beginner writers, as well as to old hands.

3. At LMFAW the organisation is promoted through libraries and other clubs and societies, and new members are welcomed into a happy friendly atmosphere. There is no judgment for those whose skills are as yet unsure, only encouragement and kindness.

Aims 4) and 5) are the responsibility of the State Committee, and I believe we are attempting to honour them.

For number 6) I do think LMFAW is trying, with caution, to move in this direction.

To sum up, I think that the Lake Macquarie Branch of The Fellowship of Australian Writers NSW embodies all ideals that the founders wanted, and I am immensely proud to be a member.

At a writing group

Linda Visman

I'm sitting with my writing group
listening to a presentation
I'm feeling disappointed 'cos
I don't need this information.

The topic deals with writing but
it's not relevant to my situation.
Copy-writing's not my thing –
it nullifies my imagination.

Most of our meetings are really great
and give plenty of inspiration,
but now and then it's not for me
so I lose my concentration.

And I write a poem instead!

The coffee break

Rob West

"Good morning!" Big smile. "How can I help you?"

"Hi. Just coffee please. Do you have lactose-free milk?"

She turns to barista. "Do we have lactose-free milk?"

"Yes."

"Yes, we do." Another smile.

"OK, I'll have a small flat white coffee on lactose-free."

"What size? Small, medium or large?"

"Small please."

"And, have it here or take away?"

"Have it here please. And can I have two shots."

"In a cup or a takeaway container?"

"In a cup. I said I will have it here."

"Some people have it here, but they want it in a takeaway container."

"OK." He turns to companion. "What do you want?"

"Er, just a normal flat white, in a cup."

"Medium size?"

"No, small please."

"Lactose free milk?"

"No, normal milk."

She turns to barista. "A medium normal flat white in a cup."

Barista (puzzled frown): "Do they want one coffee or two?"

Me: "Two please. Mine was lactose free flat white, IN A CUP, hers was ... Oh look, just give us a pot of tea? Two cups."

All meetings of our branch have some sort of emphasis on food, tea and coffee - hence the theme of this poem.

Critique meetings: thick skin? Thin skin? An honest approach

Alison Ferguson

As writers (or performers, or artists) we cannot avoid feedback. Actors, musicians, and stand-up comedians use rehearsal as a way to channel feedback into a better performance. In the final production, the feedback is immediate as the audience laughs and cries in all the right places. Painters and sculptors sketch, experiment with colour on their palettes, and re-work to achieve their best. When their creative piece is exhibited or made available for sale, they too can receive direct feedback.

Writers also go through processes of editing and revision. However, for us, the feedback on the final work is less immediate. Our readers are distant from us, so we can't watch their reactions. We excitedly submit our story to a competition or our novel to a publisher and then face a long wait. Quite possibly we never hear back as to the outcome let alone receive any feedback as to why our writing wasn't successful in a competition or didn't pique the interest of a publisher. In the happy event of being published (whether through a commercial publisher or by self-publishing), how can we evaluate readers' reactions to our work? For example, how representative are readers' online comments and, if our sales figures are small, how much can we attribute to difficulties in marketing as opposed to the quality of our writing?

One solution is to obtain constructive criticism before submission. However, it's possible that the reason we express our creativity through writing rather than performance may well be the fear of direct and immediate feedback. We all have some degree of experience in receiving feedback, starting from childhood, progressing through education and into our workplace. Those experiences will have left their mark. Feelings of unfairness, or not being understood may have resulted in a psychic skin so thick that we find it difficult to really listen to suggestions. On the other hand, we may be so thin skinned that we perceive any comment negatively.

Well-known author Neil Gaiman once said, 'I suspect that most authors don't really want criticism, not even constructive criticism. They want straight-out, unabashed, unashamed, fulsome, informed, naked praise, arriving by the shipload every fifteen minutes or so.'

He may well be right (!), but we also learn how to be better writers if we open our writing to constructive critique from our fellow writers. The shiploads of praise can come later ... For this reason, one of the main activities of our FAW branch is critiquing each other's work in progress.

A critique story

KJ Mair

The room seemed to shake.

'The monster stepped closer and closer. As it did it grew bigger and bigger. Details formed, of teeth so long they couldn't fit in its mouth. Of claws sharper than the most worked over school pencil. Of –'

The lights flickered.

"Could you stop there please. You ran a little ahead of yourself," said the lady with rather large glasses. Her name tag flashed in the light – Gale.

Across the table, I saw a woman with a flashy red scarf squint down at the page and mutter, "School pencil?"

The group at the table said nothing. Though there was a glance or two I couldn't interpret. One of the men frowned. Gale hissed, "Agatha!"

Gale pushed her glasses back up her nose as she smiled at me. "We have a certain way of doing things here."

I shrank back down into my seat. Damn. Damn. I've just joined and already screwed up.

"Of course. Sorry," I said.

I briefly imagined snatching all the papers off them and making a running leap off the balcony. *Surely, my leg wouldn't break from this high up*?

"You've got nothing to be sorry for. This is your first time. Now, how this works is, we find that hearing someone else read aloud your work really ..."

I was really trying to listen. Truly. But I saw something move from within the shadows of the inner room. Something hulking. Something with eyes that glowed an unnatural green as it stared me down.

"... so Agatha will read yours, since she showed such an interest in it. Won't you, Agatha?"

Agatha raised an eyebrow and twisted her lips in such a way that suggested she would rather not, but was too polite to say.

From the other room, the monster growled. I jumped, but no one else seemed to notice.

Agatha cleared her throat in an exaggerated way. So much so, I was afraid a literal frog would leap out. But after tightening her scarf and smacking her lips, she began –

'The little girl never believed the lies her parents told her. Monsters were real.

And she was going to prove it ...'

On and on Agatha went.

To be honest I really wasn't listening. Instead, I was looking at the faces around me. Trying to gauge a reaction. But they were stoic. Expressions flat, as their eyes scanned line by line something I'm realising I should never have shared. I should have kept it all in the confines of my skull and never typed a word of it. My imagination should have been locked up, with any possibility of parole crossed out.

Behind me, I could feel the monster's breath along the back of my neck. It sent starbursts of cold and heat up and down my spine. I was sweating. My heart racing. Hands shaking.

Agatha approached the end. Her voice fitting the flow.

‘Suddenly, despite its growling, its teeth and very long claws, the little girl stood up and hugged the monster.

The monster struggled at first, but then relaxed. It had never known defeat like this before.’

There was a silence. A long one.

Has anyone dropped dead at one of these meetings before?

And then, “Wow.”

Surprisingly, it came from Agatha herself. “You might need to work on some on your similes.” She smiled, big and open. “But crap, kid, you can tell a good story.”

Gale rolled her eyes. “Swearing aside. I think Agatha is right on the money. You did really well. And you said this was your first?”

I couldn’t talk, so I nodded.

“Well done. And how did it feel to hear it read out loud?”

Behind me, the monster vanished like it was never there. It probably wasn’t.

“It felt ...”

Frightening.

Monstrous.

Heroic.

“... educational. I really learned some things about myself.”

Section 4

Who we are

We're writers – but that means many things. In this section, we explore the diverse voices, backgrounds, and experiences that shape us. Writing is part of our identity, but so is the journey we take to become ourselves.

Presidents of LMFAW

2000	Anna Scott
2001	Alice Sinclair
2002	Alice Sinclair
2003	Nola McCarthy
2004	Nola McCarthy
2005	Wendy Alexander
2006	Beth Parnaby
2007	Terry Colling
2008	Lis Gerrard
2009	Sophie Bush
2010	Sophie Bush
2011	Jan Mitchell
2012	Jan Mitchell
2013	Linda Visman
2014	Linda Visman
2015	Ken Humphries
2016	Alison Ferguson
2017	Kristen Mair
2018	Kristen Mair
2019	Kristen Mair
2020	Pam Garfoot
2021	Pam Garfoot
2022	Irina Frolova
2023	Sandra Boyd
2024	Pam Garfoot / Sandra Boyd
2025	Sandra Boyd

Biography of Rina Robinson: a founding member

Pam Garfoot

Rina Robinson has been with our group since its very beginning. Indeed, she was, along with Anna Scott, instrumental in getting the Lake Macquarie Branch of FAW up and running.

Born in the United Kingdom, Rina was drawn to work on stage and screen, to be a principal dancer in pantomime, and to do stage work with puppets. Her extensive career as a performer brought her to Australia in 1954 and she never returned to live in Britain. She lived for some time in the Sydney area before moving to Lake Macquarie.

As time went on Rina was able to focus on another of her creative interests: writing. This she did in other FAW groups (in Sydney and Newcastle) and in a U3A group, before the Lake Macquarie FAW was set up in 2000. At the very first public meeting of the group, in August of that year, she was elected Vice President. From then onwards, until at least 2008, Rina held various positions on the committee (including social coordinator, catering officer, assistant treasurer, and editorial committee officer for the Branch's magazine *Macquarie Muse / MacMuse*). She attended virtually every Committee meeting, her name appearing over and over in the surviving committee minutes.

At first Rina wrote under a male pseudonym for truckers' magazines. She soon began writing poetry, short stories and novels. *Tarnished Threads: Australian country town tales,* Rina's debut novella, features her art work on its cover. A second novella, *Lily for the Living: Australian country tales*, and two fantasy novels, *Summer Sorcery* and *Singing*

Maiden, followed. An engaging children's book, *Alphabet Antics*, is both written and illustrated by Rina, as is her book of poems, *Views & Visions*. Many other examples of her work have been published in magazines and anthologies. As if all this was not enough, for some years Rina also exhibited her artwork at Lake Macquarie's Dobell Art Festival.

Despite the demands of Committee work, Rina managed to pursue her writing projects throughout her time with our group. After stepping down from the committee she still regularly attended the group's meetings, actively contributing to discussions. Group writing exercises were enhanced by her delightful pieces – memoir, poetry, and short story – and the unique perspectives she offered freely to others in the group.

In 2015 Rina received the FAW(NSW) Distinguished Service Award. It is only recently that health issues have prevented Rina from being so active in the group.

In early 2024 Lake Macquarie FAW members were delighted to be able to wish Rina a happy 100th birthday. Some members attended her birthday celebrations, where they heard even more about her amazing and creative life – not least of all that she is a mother of two, a grandmother of three, and a great grandmother of seven.

Without the hard work Rina put in and her collaboration with other committee members, the Lake Macquarie FAW would not be the strong vibrant group it is today.

Broken chords

Rina Robinson

The Dancer
She leaves her chair
And moves to the centre of the room.
She takes a step.
Then another: then totters some more.
It is not pretty.
But in her mind
The music swells and she soars
Graceful, beautiful,
A ballerina again.

The Singer
He tries to rise
From the wheelchair's irreverent constraint,
A patchwork of harmony
At last, before the swan song.
His crestfallen aspect
Is reversed for a moment.
The baritone voice surprises,
Rich, powerful,
The song he remembers.

The Judge

He raises his arm,

A tangled salute to the day.

A haunted Solomon,

Yesterday's arbiter of power.

Yet bedevilled brains

Overtake the apathy

And face the jury.

Harmonious verdict,

His future epitaph.

* This poem was awarded a Commendation Prize in the Roland Robinson Literary Award for 1996 and appeared in the anthology, *Lines from a Lakeside City* the same year. It was reprinted in *HPA Magazine*, issue 4 2019.

Image by Pam Garfoot. As it appeared in *Beneath the Surface.*

Fellowship of Australian Writers NSW Inc.

Distinguished Service Award

Rina Robinson

Rina Robinson has long been an active member of the Lake Macquarie Branch of the Fellowship of Australian Writers (NSW) and has spent a lifetime in creative pursuits of many sorts.

Born in the United Kingdom, at age 12 Rina began a career on stage and screen as principal dancer in pantomime. Soon she added variety shows and summer theatre seasons to her repertoire. She toured the UK and the continent performing a sister act with Elaine Peters.

In 1954 Rina travelled solo to Brisbane on the maiden voyage of P&O's *Iberia*. After her arrival she was invited to join a concert party touring Queensland. Hers was a popular act and included dancing with a marionette. Rina married Dennis Robinson and continued with the Theatre Royal. Rina and Dennis relocated to Sydney, with Dennis joining the act. They featured on Don Lane's and Graham Kennedy's television shows, as well as in overseas performances. Acting performances on film and television, as well as tutoring in speech and drama, added to Rina's long list of accomplishments.

Writing was the next creative pursuit Rina tackled. When she first started writing she did so under a male pseudonym for a truckers' magazine. She soon began writing poetry, short stories and novels. *Tarnished Threads: Australian country town tales,* Rina's debut novella, features her art work on its cover. A second novella, *Lily for the Living: Australian country tales,* and two fantasy novels, *Summer Sorcery* and *Singing Maiden,* have followed. An engaging children's book, *Alphabet Antics,* is both written and illustrated by Rina, as is her book of poems, *Views & Visions.* Many other works have been published in magazines and anthologies. Until very recently Rina exhibited her artwork at Lake Macquarie's Dobell Art Festival.

Rina was a founding member of the Lake Macquarie Branch of the Fellowship of Australian Writers (NSW), and attended its first meeting in late 2000. She has continued to be a member throughout the intervening 15 years. Rina was Vice President of the group for two years. She also served on the Executive Committee for some years, holding a variety of different positions: social coordinator, catering officer, assistant treasurer, and editorial committee officer for the Branch's magazine *MacMuse.* At 91 years of age she still regularly attends the group's meetings, actively contributing to discussions. Group writing exercises are enhanced by her delightful pieces - memoir, poetry, and short story - and the unique perspectives she offers freely to others in the group.

Written by Pam Garfoot

2015

Photos:

Left: Rina dancing at her 100th birthday

Below: Rina and her DSA.

Numbers & names

Sandra Boyd

Over the years, we have seen a lot of duplication in names - some even members at the same time, like the 3 Carols!

First names

10 Anne/Anekes/Anita/Anna/Annie
10 Catherine/Cate/Kath/Katherine/Kathryn/Kathy
10 Marie/Marian/Marilyn/Mary/Maryjane
8 Margaret/Margarita
7 Chris/Chrissy/Christine/Christy/Kris/Kristen
7 Lin/Linda
6 Jan/Janene/Janette/Janine
5 Helen
5 Jo/Joan
5 Robin/Robyn
5 Wendy
4 Carol/Carolyn
4 Jean/Jeanne/Jeanette
4 Richard/Rick
4 Rose/Roslyn/Rosemary
4 Sue/Suellen/Susan/Suzanne
4 Toni/Tony/Anthony

Surnames

4 Edwards
4 Lang
3 Boyd
3 Bryant
3 Carr
3 Fenton
3 Hall
3 McCarthy
3 Morgan
3 Taylor

Some of our general meeting speakers

Date	*Name*	*Topic*
4/02/2006	Julie Simpson	
4/03/2006	Penny Hall	Writing for teenagers
1/04/2006	Beth Parnaby	Layering the Senses
6/05/2006	Ruth Colman	Punctuation
3/06/2006	Wendy	Characterisation
5/08/2006	Brenda Bryant	Performance: Little Somethings
2/09/2006	Jan Dean	
3/03/2007	Dorothea Twomey	
7/07/2007	Tony	Poetry Appreciation
4/08/2007	Dorothea Twomey	Critiquing Activities
2/09/2007		Poets on Wheels?
6/10/2007	Magdalena Ball	
1/03/2008	Dorothea Twomey	Show me a Character
5/04/2008	Louise Berry	Critiquing Activities
5/04/2008	Sophie Bush	Publishing
3/05/2008		AGM, Alice Sinclair Results
7/03/2009	Jo Tregellis	Free Verse
4/04/2009	Louise Berry	Emotions
2/05/2009	Kathryn Anderson	
3/06/2009	Jo Tregellis	Tanka
4/07/2009	Rina Robinson	Dialogue
1/08/2009		Submissions for MacMuse
5/09/2009	Sophie Bush	Editing
3/10/2009	Linda Visman	Keeping the Voice
7/11/2009		Opening Paragraph
1/05/2010	Linda Visman	Talk Sentence
5/06/2010	Gail Hennessy	Book Launch
3/07/2010	Louise Berry	Observation
7/08/2010	Magdalena Ball	
4/09/2010	Dael Allison	Nature Writing
2/10/2010	Linda Brooks	Alice Sinclair Winners

Date	*Name*	*Topic*
6/11/2010	Rina Robinson	Pantomine
4/12/2010		Pantomine Performance
4/02/2012	Magdalena Ball	
14/03/2014	Chris Allen	Writing adventures and action thrillers
10/07/2015	Claire Pasvolsky	On Creativity
14/05/2016	Magdalena Ball	
9/07/2016	Frances Robertson	Editing
13/08/2016	Cate Plink	Competition Rules
10/09/2016	Jan Mitchell	Creating e-books
08/10/2016	Linda Visman	Blogging
08/09/2018	kaz Delaney	The State of the Industry, and the Craft of Writing
13/08/2022	Lee Christine	
19/09/2022	Susan Francis	
12/11/2022		ASC Awards
11/02/2023		Failure to Launch
13/05/2023	Jaye Ford	
10/06/2023	Cate Plink	Voice
10/08/2024	Jan Mitchell	Proofreading
7/09/2024	Steve Shipley	AI
12/10/2024	Kristen Mair	The Basics of Writing
8/02/2025	Ned Stephenson	Writing for Competitions
8/03/2025	Natalie Murray	RomComs
12/04/2025		Festival Practice
10/05/2025	Sandra Boyd	Write, write and write some more
14/06/2025		Skills Showcase
9/08/2025		Pantsing vs Planning: a light-hearted debate

Vale to these previous members ...

Alice Sinclair (2003)
Anita Richardson (2022)
Anna Scott
Dawn van Koeverden
Gail Hennessy (2023)
Greg Bowen
Irene Kelly (2023)
Jeanette Brewster (2007)
Jo Hanrahan
Jo Tregellis (2020)
Joan McCarthy (2024)
Keith Davey
Lesley Mansfield
Margaret Young (2023)
Marie Every-Burns
Marie Walther/Henery
Mel Sommers
Nola McCarthy
Patricia (Trish) Withers
Tony Mays (2007)

Collated by Pam Garfoot and Linda Visman

and others we don't know about.

Stories don't end when the book does

Linda Visman

Have you ever finished a short story or a novel and couldn't get the characters out of your head?

Have you imagined what might have happened after the story finished?

With a good story and well-realised characters, I think it happens quite often. I know it has to me.

I suppose that is why there is so much fan fiction written, and why readers love book series.

They don't want to lose those characters, that world, that reality created by the author. They want the story to go on.

Think Harry Potter. To many of her readers, J.K. Rowlings' imaginary character has become just as real as their own family and friends. He is someone they may know even better than those real people. It just happens that Harry, together with his own friends and foes, lives somewhere else.

They dwell in a different reality. It is a reality that has a door from our own that we can enter at will, or which can spill for a time into our own reality through the magic key of reading.

Why do some characters and their worlds become so real, when others do not? Why do we want to stay with some when we can't even get to know others – or want to?

That to me is another magic. The magic created by a sensitive, observant and creative writer. Such writers do not necessarily create great works of literature (as defined by high-brow literary critics).

What they do create are real worlds occupied by real people, with real feelings and desires, hopes and dreams, challenges and triumphs. Characters with whom the reader develops empathy, a feeling of one-ness.

It's no wonder we don't want to leave the book – in a way it is our own life we have been reading, or that of people we have become close to. We want to know more.

Do you ever identify with or become close to characters in the books you read?

Writers' Showcase 2013

Linda Visman & Christina Batey

The Lake Macquarie FAW Writers' Showcase was held on 31st August 2013 at the Lake Macquarie Performing Arts Centre, Warners Bay. It featured a glittering list of guest speakers, all of whom currently live, have lived, or have been inspired in their writing by Lake Macquarie and surrounding regions. The aim was to showcase the writing talent in the region and familiarise the public with their work.

The Showcase was introduced and closed by Lake Macquarie FAW President, Linda Visman, and officially opened by State Member for Lake Macquarie, Mr Greg Piper MLA.

The day kicked off with a panel hosted by Magdalena Ball that included Jaye Ford, Judy Johnson and Beryl Mullard. They held a lively discussion about writing, story ideas, and the long, hard road to publication. Their enthusiasm and knowledge inspired many questions from the audience and provided rich insights.

The most encouraging thing for many of the audience was that successful authors began with just a simple idea that they stuck with. All had to juggle their writing with nose-to-the-grindstone jobs before they could afford the luxury of being able to write full-time.

The Showcase covered almost every genre and style of writing. Poetry was represented by bush poet and FAW Lake Macquarie member, Carol Heuchan, and by contemporary poets Jean Kent and Judy Johnson. These ladies all enjoy both national and international success, having won many awards and prizes for their poetry. Jean and Carol both chose a poem to present to the audience. They were simple, beautiful and very moving. Carol also did a wonderful job as MC for the day.

Younger readers were treated to very entertaining talks by Kaz Delaney and Lake Macquarie FAW's very own Linda Visman and Christina Batey. Within our group, we have written books for every age group from beginning readers to Crossover YA and Adult, as well as poetry and non-fiction. Rina Robinson, one of the founders of Lake Macquarie FAW branch, also spoke. She has written fantasy and contemporary short stories for adults and older teenagers as well as writing and illustrating picture books for young children.

Non-fiction fans and aspiring writers in the audience were also entertained and informed with talks from representatives of the Wangi Wangi Sailing Club, who have spent over five years compiling a beautiful book on the history of the club. It is not surprising that our beautiful lake is the source of rich inspiration.

Another writer, who has enjoyed adventure on the high seas is Lake Macquarie FAW's Jan Mitchell. Jan spoke about her collection of articles, written over the years for various magazines and now compiled into a fascinating account of her travels. Beryl Mullard spoke about her deeply researched and comprehensive book on the history of Morisset and also other history writing projects.

Linda Brooks's signature humour entertained, with her tales of dealing with her son's Asperger's Syndrome. The inspiration and good advice continued to flow from guests such as Debbie Robson, Karen Davey-Phillip, and FAW Lake Macquarie members Elizabeth Horwitz and Tony Lang.

The Local Writers Showcase was a great success for the Lake Macquarie FAW's organising committee and helpers. It was an altogether uplifting and thought-provoking day, leaving all of us revitalised, inspired and ready to go put some powerful words together. The single drawback was that most attendees were themselves writers, or aspiring writers, and although they relished the information provided by published authors, not many readers were in evidence.

Carol Heuchan, M.C.

Books for sale in the foyer.

writing group

Irina Frolova

writing festival
we talk to the audience —
Why Write

on the Committee
a year goes by reading
the minutes

25th year —
we carry on
writing

Lake Macquarie welcomes Poets on Wheels

Press Release written by Linda Visman, 2007

The Lake Macquarie Fellowship of Australian Writers will host the fifteenth annual Poets on Wheels tour on Sunday, the 2nd of September in Toronto.

The tour is organised by the Poets Union of Australia, whose aim is to encourage the dissemination and appreciation of poetry throughout the country. Following a week-long tour of the Central Coast of New South Wales, this group of eminent poets will conclude their tour in Toronto.

The poets will conduct a workshop at Toronto Library from 5pm to 7pm, at which they will discuss poems brought in by local poets. After an hour's break for dinner there will be Poetry Readings at Toronto Workers Club from 8pm to 10pm. At this, the visiting poets will read their poems. Local poets are also invited to bring in and read their own poetry.

There will be a cash prize of $40 for the Best Local Poem, and certificates will be awarded to the Most Highly Commended of the local poets.

If you are a poet, a would-be poet or just interested in hearing great poetry, you are invited to participate in this rare opportunity to work with some of Australia's best poets, in a relaxing and fun-filled atmosphere. Even if you have never put pen to paper, you can be assured of a great learning experience and an entertaining evening. So come and join us.

The entry fee for the workshop will be $5, payable on the night. Entry to the Readings will be by gold coin donation.

Those who wish to participate in the workshop need to register their names by calling Lake Macquarie FAW President, Terry Colling. They are also asked to bring writing materials to the workshop. Those wishing to read their work at the evening Reading should bring ten copies of their poems for distribution at the workshop.

NOTE FROM LINDA 17 December 2024

This is the event our group hosted for Poets on Wheels on 2nd Sept 2007 when Terry Colling was president and I was secretary. I attended the workshop & Poetry Reading where I read two of my poems (I can't remember if any other member/s attended). I won the Best Local Poem prize with my Northern Territory poem "Petrol for Sex".

Petrol for sex

Linda Visman

Her body moves in rhythm to his thrusts.
Eyes closed, she's in another world,
unaware of what is happening to her.
Twelve years old, a child –
the focus of his warped desires.
Should be in school,
but it never was important
even when she was aware.
No future anyway. Why bother?

Finished, the old man pushes her aside.
She whimpers, and reaches out
for the can of petrol on the sand
her payment.
Dull eyes momentarily gleam
as she holds it to her face and inhales,
killing a few million more brain cells.
But she doesn't know about that –
And he doesn't care.

Member achievements – just a taste

Pam Garfoot

People join writing groups for a variety of reasons. Most would say that at least one of those reasons is to help them become a better writer. So, it is good to have some evidence that members have, indeed, improved their writing. What better proof than success in competitions and having some writing published (as whole books, contributions to anthologies, or in some other form)?

The list of our member achievements is long, but below are some of the major ones achieved while these members were part of our group.

Competition successes:

Over multiple years many of our members have been finalists in the Newcastle Herald Short Story Competition - Linda Brooks, Vicky Norton, Kristen Mair, Christy Lutz, Anita Richardson, Pam Garfoot, Bronwyn MacRitchie, Thelma Wawrzonek, Olga Korlevic, Ned Stephenson.

Kristen received special judges' mention and second prize on a couple of memorable occasions.

In 2025 Alison Ferguson won the competition, with Ned and Kristen being finalists.

Members have also often been successful in our own blind-judged ***Alice Sinclair Memorial Writing Competition***: Patricia Withers, Marie Every-Burns, Lesley Mansfield, Gail Hennessy, Linda Brooks, Kristen Mair, Victoria Norton, Rina Robinson, Jan Mitchell, Linda Visman, Ned Stephenson, Black Crow Walking, George Graves, Bronwyn MacRitchie, Irina Frolova.

Over multiple years members have been included in the ***Seniors' Stories anthology***: Alison Ferguson, John Franks, Cate Plink, Jan Mitchell, Alana Henderson, Linda Visman.

2002 Rina Robinson, Jo Tregellis, Marian Morgan, Marie Walther (all commended in poetry competitions), Alice Sinclair (Max Harris Literary Award, commended in Far North Coast FAW Poetry Competition), Tony Mays (commended in a short story competition)

2005 Wendy Alexander, Jo Tregellis (both awarded in the Denis Butler Competition, Wendy Alexander in the Roland Robinson Literary Award)

2006 Wendy Alexander, Patricia Withers (both awarded in the Roland Robinson Literary Award)

2007 Jo Tregellis (FAW Macarthur Region Literary Competition Free Verse Section)

2008 Linda Visman (Henry Lawson Festival Competition Verse Section), Patricia Withers (FAW North Shore Poetry Competition)

2014 Vicky Norton (awarded in the Eastwood Hills Branch FAW Literary Competition), Helen Marshall (commended in QRRRWN competition), Pam Garfoot (winner Queensland Family History Society Book of 2014 competition)

2015 Pam Garfoot ('Who was Harry Hartog' Competition finalist, Highly Commended in the Port Stephens Examiner Literature Award), Linda Visman (winner of the NSW Regional FAW Newsletter Award)

2016 Pam Greene and Linda Visman (Morisset District Show writing award), Margaret Leggatt (shortlisted in Flash500 Competition), Pam Garfoot (Port Stephens Examiner Literature Award)

2018 Alison Ferguson (shortlisted in Sisters in Crime Scarlet Stiletto Award, also NSW Seniors Card Short Story Award), Elizabeth Horwitz (received a Shortland Award for her work with Hunter Professional Arts), Tony Lang (Best of Times Short Story Competition)

2019 Alison Ferguson (shortlisted Newcastle Short Story Award, shortlisted in Brio Books Fantastica Competition, winner of the Margaret Cech Award for Science Fiction and Fantasy), Janette Ellis (Hunter Writers' Centre Grieve Competition)

2020 Alison Ferguson (shortlisted Queensland Writers' Centre Publishable Program for Emerging Writers, shortlisted Queensland Writers Centre Adaptable Competition), Kristen Mair (longlisted The Big Issue's Fiction edition, shortlisted for the Heroines Women's Writing Prize and Anthology), Sandi Boyd (third place Odyssey House Short Story Competition)

2021 Irina Frolova (runner-up Deborah Cass Prize for Writing), Alison Ferguson (shortlisted Marjorie Barnard Award)

2022 Kristen Mair (shortlisted Scarlet Stiletto Sisters in Crime Award), Margaret Young (winner Toastmasters Humorous Speech Competition)

2023 Pam Garfoot (Joan Reese Memorial Short Story Competition, Journal Article of the Year in *Queensland Family Historian*), Kristen Mair (Sunspot Lit Rigel Writing Competition), Ned Stephenson (Sydney Hammond Memorial Short Story Competition, Stringybark Erotic Short Story Award), Bronwyn MacRitchie (awarded in Odyssey House Short Story Competition), Alana Henderson (Port Stephens Literature Award), Irina Frolova (longlisted University of Canberra Vice Chancellor's International Poetry Prize)

2024 Irina Frolova (longlisted for Heroines Anthology, longlisted Liquid Amber Press Poetry Prize), Ned Stephenson (shortlisted for Ernestine Hill Memorial Short Story Award, longlisted Sydney Hammond Memorial Short Story Competition, awarded in Stringybark Short Story Award and in Best of Times Short Story Competition)

Competitions judged:

Jan Mitchell (Hilarie Lindsay)

Pam Garfoot (Ernestine Hill Writing Competition)

Fellowship of Australian Writers NSW Inc.

Distinguished Service Award

Books published:

Here are some of the multitudes:

2011 Linda Visman *Ben's challenge*; Rina Robinson *Tarnished threads*; Christina Batey *Kicker*; Jan Mitchell *Tinker, tailor, soldier, sailor*

2013 Tony Lang *Ghosts, ghouls, God*

2014 Vicky Norton *Purple, emerald, gold*; Linda Brooks *Wings to fly;* Tony Lang *Magic mist*; Vicky Norton and Helen Marshall *Who ate the cake*

2015 Jan Mitchell *Two in a top hat* and *Crossings in Realitas*

2016 Carol Heuchan *Petunia and the pony*

2017 Alice Ferguson *A gentleman's daughter*

2018 Tony Lang *What the Bible really says about women* and *A kangaroo loose in Scotland*; Linda Visman *Thursday's child*

2019 Jan Mitchell *Hear the ocean sing*

2020 Jan Mitchell *Food for eyes*; Sandra Joy *Salvation Through the Gift of Help*

2021 Alison Ferguson *Maiden manoeuvres, Dearest daughter* and *Widow's wake*

2022 Alison Ferguson *Grey nomad*; Sandra Joy *Life: a variant of adventures*; Tony Lang *The Channel Bank and other verse*; Steve Shipley *False trust*

2023 Pam Garfoot *Capricorn drover*; Olga Korlevic *Nello's yellow excavator* and *The art gallery of dreams*; Joan McCarthy *Travelling first class*; Sandra Joy (as author) the *Happy Helper* series; Sandra Joy (as publisher) *Life's toolbox anthologies*; Cate Plink *Jacinta in the mirror*; John Franks *Echoes*

2024 Olga Korlevic *Not what you think*; Joan McCarthy *The world through my eyes*; Wayne Russell *Shattered falls*; Steve Shipley *False start;* Cate Plink *Tanya haunted*

Short stories, articles, poems, book reviews and numerous other pieces were published in newsletters, magazines, anthologies, and numerous other places. For several years the *Hunter Professional Arts Magazine* was one of the places where many of our members were published. And, of course, our group published two impressive anthologies of its own - *Beneath the surface* and *Out of the shadows* - where several members made it into print.

The following are the front and back cover of the member catalogue created by Bronwyn MacRitchie in 2023.

Perhaps one day we can create an updated member catalogue. Previous / members can email us to have your book included.

I ***Presentations given:***

2015 Members gave a panel presentation at the Newcastle Writers Festival

2016 Jan Mitchell presented at Newcastle Writers Festival

2018 Linda Visman did an author 'pop up' session in Millthorpe, NSW

2019 Margaret Young read at the Blue Room Poets anthology launch; Four members gave a panel presentation at the Newcastle Writers Festival on "The making of a book"

2022 Sandra Joy gave talks to preschoolers on being 'Happy helpers'; members participated in two panel presentations at the Write Here! Festival; Pam Garfoot presented to primary students on her grandfather at Gallipoli using her book *Making them real*; and members (led by Joan McCarthy and featuring Linda Visman's title poem) participated in the *On the Rocks* event at Lake Macquarie Libraries

2023 and **2024** members gave panel presentations at the Lake Macquarie Write Here! Festival

2023 Members were on a panel at the Maitland Indie Festival; John Franks spoke at various venues; Alison Ferguson was a guest panellist at Brisbane GenreCon, and guest at Brisbane Writers Festival, Mudgee Readers Festival and Maitland Indie Festival

2024 Members were on a discussion panel at the Write Here! Festival

The messenger

Alice Sinclair

This story was written by Alice in the first two years of the LMFAW

My mother always understood my great love of trees. When other children were cherishing dogs and cats, she had always known better than to thrust these poor creatures into my care. Instead, she encouraged me to plant my trees and kept me happy with a steady supply of watering cans.

Not long before her death, she had insisted that I should return to the country town where I had grown up and where an old aunt had recently died and left me her home. I made the promise carelessly, not intending to move. It wasn't until I was left alone that I realised the wisdom of it.

From the first sighting of my aunt's old home, I knew I would be happy there. A shelter of leaves welcomed me with a great rustling. Lawn mowers and plastic rakes hadn't been particularly active, the yard was warm with fallen colour. The lady-like jacaranda beckoned me to her shade, and the street-wise eucalypt towered protection over the crab apple and the stolid lillypillies. I greeted them all according to their nature and the bond was sealed.

The people in the town knew who I was and nodded pleasantly to me in passing. Some I spoke to, remembering them from boyhood, but generally, I kept to myself, preferring solitude to idle chit chat. This included my relationship with neighbours: I didn't go out of my way to speak to them. I was a little taken aback therefore, when a willy wagtail type female accosted me over the side fence. I was enjoying my morning paper under quiet shade when a voice like sharp tin jagged my ears.

“Now that you’ve settled in, I suppose you’ll be getting rid of some of these trees!” Not a request mind you, a bald statement, uttered in tones bordering on smug satisfaction.

I looked at the small head, just visible over the palings, and replied, “ No!” in a voice which I hoped would baulk any further conversation on the subject.

“We thought you would. ”

“ YOU thought he would!” From a male voice somewhere behind her.

“They’re a nuisance, you know. Their leaves and bits of branch — in windy weather.” Her voice bounced along the palings as she spoke, to indicate the offenders. The trees rustled their own opinions. “God told me to tell you that He would like them removed.”

“God who?” I didn’t comprehend the vastness of her meaning.

“There-is-only-one-God!” The words were evenly spaced and accented.

God? Godfrey, Goddard?

“I’m sorry,” I mumbled, “I haven’t met many people from about here. I’ve been busy, you know, moving things.”

“Aren’t you a Christian?”

Good Lord! She couldn’t mean THAT God! “You mean God as in heaven?”

“There-is-only-one-God,” she repeated, more deliberately this time.

“Yes, well, I suppose there is. But what has He got to do with my trees?”

“He doesn’t want them in your yard. He created big trees to grow in the bush, not in backyards. Backyards are for vegetables and flowers.”

“You don’t say.” I’m not normally a nasty person, being plumpish by nature, but I was beginning to feel a bit miffed – somewhere between a sense of good manners and the need to tell her to piss off “and take her God with her.” Good manners won out as my mother would have wanted.

“I think God loves the big trees that grow in my yard and the vegetables and flowers that grow in yours.” I kept my voice low and kind. She was obviously a couple of pretzels short of a party.

“No! That’s not right at all. He told me He wants the trees removed, or at least lopped to fence height.”

“Well, He’s going to be very disappointed!” Good manners were beginning to fray around the edges. “I’m not touching those trees and that’s final!” The trees continued to wave their branches about.

“He’ll strike you down with pestilence for not doing as He asks.”

“And I’ll strike you down with a shovel if I see you anywhere near my trees!” Not a good start to neighbourly relations, but in certain circumstances one has to be firm.

The next morning there was a quiet knock at the back door. A strange man was standing on the mat marked WELCOME, a purchase made in a moment of weakness, a plate of pikelets in his hands.

“Ruby sent these for your morning tea, by way of apology for yesterday. She gets carried away sometimes.”

By now, I was feeling embarrassed too, and a bit guilty. I should have taken time to explain about the bond I had with trees.

"Thank you very much. There was really no need," I said, indicating the pikelets. "I was as much to blame as anyone. Come in. My name is Barry by the way. I don't think we got around to introducing ourselves yesterday."

"No. Things got off to a bad start. I'm Sid, Ruby's husband."

We shook hands, over the pikelets. He seemed a placid sort of chap, not given to unnecessary words.

"Would you like a cup of tea, Sid?"

"Better not, thanks. Ruby starts prayers about now."

"She prays a lot, does she Sid?"

"A fair bit."

I looked at Sid and Sid looked back at me, and we understood that no further words were necessary. I tipped the pikelets into a dish, dusted the crumbs off the plate and handed it back to him. He thanked me and trudged off home.

Things quietened down a bit after that, although every few days I was regaled over the fence with a few more divine revelations about trees and their great need to live in the bush with their friends. Apparently, God can be quite chatty when he lets Himself go.

Ruby was certain she was on a dead set path to heaven. "I'm sure where I'm going! Straight into the arms of glory," as she stared in the general direction of the sun. I thought only trains and Catholics could be quite so definite about their destination, but didn't say so. I was learning to tolerate Ruby's eccentricities and Sid seemed to appreciate my new attitude.

Only once was I inveigled into a prayer session. In spite of strong intentions, I can sometimes be very soft. I suppose it comes from living alone with my mother for all those years.

It was a coolish morning, too cold really to be sitting outside, and Ruby made the hot scones and cream sound so enticing that I weakened. She didn't actually mention prayers although I was prepared for a few muttered words of grace.

Sid looked surprised, even shocked, when I said, "Thank you, Ruby, that would be lovely. I'll just wash my hands.' He called me over to the fence. Ruby had scuttled inside, singing.

Sid kept his voice low, "Are you sure you want to come in, mate? You don't have to, you know."

"I know, Sid, but being neighbourly won't hurt me. And the scones sound lovely."

"It's not the scones I'm thinking about. Please yourself. But don't forget I warned you!"

I laughed. Silly me! I should have listened!

For two hours she went on. She prayed for everything and everyone, alive and dead. I lost track after a time. My knees began to pain and my back ached. I had nothing to lean on. Sid, obviously used to the performance, had rested his elbows and eventually his head, on the back of a chair. He looked too relaxed to be awake. I prodded him. He slipped sideways and snorted. Ruby glared at him, not missing one prayerful word. When the final 'Amen' petered out I couldn't believe it was over. I had trouble standing, my knees kept giving way.

"I don't think I'll have that cup of tea, thanks Ruby. I'll just take a couple of scones if that's all right and head off home." I'd been through the agony, why not have the reward.

"Are you sure, Barry? We could have had a lovely talk over a cup of tea, couldn't we Sid?"

"Yeah!" The expression on Sid's face required no words.

I didn't see much of Sid for a while. I think he was probably too embarrassed after the debacle of the morning tea. God seemed to be encouraged by my visit though and continued to pass on His little messages, more or less on a daily basis.

I wondered how He had time to manage the universe if He was so fussy about details. I mentioned this fact to Ruby and she promised to pray for me. I would have preferred God not to be so constantly reminded of my presence, just in case there was something in all that hell and damnation nonsense.

Although I didn't see much of Sid I could always hear him pottering in the garden. He seemed to be doing a lot of digging. Quite a lot actually.

When I was sure Ruby wasn't watching I had a bit of a sticky beak through the palings; country life was beginning to change my habits. He was digging all right, a bloody great hole about two metres long. I could only see him from the knees up, the rest of him was interred.

I watched him for a few days, from the shelter of the trees, getting more and more interested. In the end, I just had to poke my head into his vision.

"What are you digging, Sid?"

"A hole!"

I waited expectantly; but that was it. I moved up a couple of palings, commenting on the weather, making a few general attempts at conversation, anything to get him talking, but Sid ignored me, just kept on digging.

Ruby was singing in the kitchen, something that sounded like 'Deutschland Deutschland Uber Alles' — perhaps God was teaching her to sing in tongues. I didn't want her to see me so I reluctantly retreated into minding my own business. It was very puzzling though.

It must have been two or three weeks later, when I realised I hadn't heard Ruby for a while. I bumped into Sid down the street. He looked quite happy with himself.

"Haven't seen Ruby for a few days, Sid?"

"Her father's not well. She's gone to look after him."

"I'm sorry to hear that. Drop in for a drink if you feel lonely. I'd be pleased to see you." You learn to tell little lies as you grow older. I knew he wouldn't come.

Time passed and Ruby still wasn't around. Mrs. Simpson, from up the street, a widow I sometimes visited for meals, had also noticed her absence.

"She's gone to look after her father," I explained.

"She'll have a job," Mrs Simpson said. "He died three years ago."

Well, that set me back a bit. It wasn't like Sid to tell lies. Perhaps it was his way of reminding me to keep my nose out of his business. So I did - for a while. Then I met him down the street again.

"Ruby not back yet, Sid?"

"Her father took another bad tum. She's staying on."

In view of Mrs. Simpson's information, 'another bad turn' seemed something of an understatement. But I said nothing, not being one to busy myself with other people's lives.

Obviously, Sid was embarrassed by Ruby's absence. I wondered if she had left him for good, gone off to some foreign place where her gifts would be appreciated. A mission field or a convent perhaps.

My mind ran on as minds tend to do. I tried to discuss the situation with the trees but they weren't all that interested. Considering Ruby's views on their existence, I suppose I could understand their attitude. Ruby still hasn't come home. No more little divine revelations or dire threats. I miss her in a way. She was always good for an argument and certainly knew how to stir life along. Another funny thing I've noticed, which I haven't bothered to mention to anyone, Sid's hole has disappeared. One day it was there, yawning into space, disrupting the scissored lawn and the next thing it had gone. Absolutely no sign of it, the lawn all smoothed over without a bump! And right in the middle of where the hole had been a young eucalypt was standing. Very strange!

Everyone in town seems to have a different view on what has happened to Ruby. Her disappearance has been the main subject of conversation for some weeks now. Certain dramatic events have been hinted at. It has even been suggested by some that the river be dragged. I thought this was going a bit far, and said so. Ruby would never do anything so dramatic as jump in the river. She wasn't the type, especially in this cold weather. Mrs. Simpson has her own ideas on the disappearance but she was always prone to sensationalism.

Sid seems to be getting on with his life quite normally. He has been on the receiving end of most people's sympathy and I know he has had a lot of free meals. Country people are a loyal bunch in time of trouble.

Publishing our anthologies

As writers, we take our anthologies seriously. For each project, an editing team is selected from the outset. Without the commitment to editing, there is no point in considering going to publication. Members' submissions must go through two critique meetings, and the final versions are sent to the author prior to publication.Titles have been decided upon through brainstorming sessions at general meetings, followed by a vote.The first two covers were designed by Scott Mair, the brother of member, Kristen Mair. This current cover was a collaboration between Eva Geerling and Leanne Deering.

Right: Our first anthology: *Beneath the Surface*, 2020.

Below: Pam Garfoot, Linda Visman, Alison Ferguson, Kristen Mair (front) at our January social 2020.

Right: Our second anthology: *Out of the Shadows*, 2023.

Publishing evolution: tracing 25 years of change with LMFAW

Deanna Lang

To help chronicle their first 25 years, the Lake Macquarie Branch of the Fellowship of Australian Writers (LMFAW) conducted a survey of members' publishing histories and experiences. This summarises the key findings of the LMFAW survey, highlighting trends over the careers of respondents and the evolution of Australia's dynamic publishing industry.

The members of the LMFAW represent a diverse range of publishing experiences as shown by the results of the survey conducted for the 25th anniversary anthology. Of the responders, 90% consider writing as a hobby while pursuing it through various avenues such as published books, articles, short stories, and poetry.

When it comes to methods of publishing, self-publishing has become the dominant approach for LMFAW members with 67% having self-published their books as independent authors. This provides writers with full creative control, the most influential factor for 90% of survey participants. However, only 55% have published more than one manuscript, indicating that self-publishing is still a learning process for some.

Traditional publishing remains an aspiration for many as receiving rejections from agents and publishers was a challenge noted by 33% of responders. Despite this, the diversity of perspectives in LMFAW has helped members navigate different publishing options over the years. Workshops and critique groups, valued highly by 80% of members, have supported their writing development.

Marketing and promoting published work stands out as the biggest post-publishing challenge according to 80% of responders. Building a readership remains difficult for 67% as promotion requires dedicated time and skills separate from writing. To overcome this, 45% have utilised online writing communities for information sharing and 33% have hired publishing professionals.

Reflecting on the changes in publishing, one long-time member remarked "traditional to self-publishing, print on demand, [and] monopolies of Amazon & the Big 5 publishers have significantly altered the landscape." Hybrid models now seem to offer the most opportunities. Emerging technologies are also revolutionising the industry at a rapid pace, demanding authors keep learning. These technologies allow writers to do more on their own, such as design, editing, managing publications, marketing, and distribution. This gives them better opportunities for self-publishing, as they are less reliant on external service providers and publishing professionals if they choose to embrace the technologies.

Collaboration has benefited some members through editorial panels for LMFAW anthologies and outside publications. One editorial veteran noticed "the editing role is very helpful for developing your own writing." Critique groups have also proven invaluable according to many responders. Mentors have guided newer authors while award recognition, though not universal, provides professional validation.

Looking ahead, most survey participants believe publishing will embrace more self-publishing and digital formats. However, some note the importance of physical events and not abandoning print-based readers. As one member advised, embracing new technologies while respecting audience preferences will serve authors well moving forward.

The LMFAW survey reveals a membership that has grown with publishing through shared highs and lows. Self-publishing has empowered members, while burdens of promotion remain. Collaborating, critiquing, and supporting one another's journeys seems integral to the group's success over 25 years. Faced with challenges, respondents demonstrate adapting skills and maintaining open-mindedness about an industry forever in transition.

Deanna Lang is an author services provider and publishing consultant with over 15 years' experience helping authors navigate the writing and publishing process.

Our group's presentations at writing festivals

Pam Garfoot

Newcastle Writers Festival

2015 "Writers groups, and the value of critique" panel presentation by Jan Mitchell, Sue Matinya, Kristen Mair (Terry Colling moderator)

2016 "All in the Family: writing family memoir" presentation by Jan Mitchell

2019 "The Making of a Book" – panel presentation by Linda Visman, Tony Lang, Pam Garfoot (Jan Mitchell moderator)

Write Here! Festival, Lake Macquarie

2022 “Why Write” panel presentation by John Franks, Sandra Joy, Irina Frolova (Alison Ferguson moderator)

2023 “Short Story Writing for Competitions and Anthologies” – panel presentation by Cate Plink, Ned Stephenson, Sandra Joy (Alison Ferguson moderator)
“Self-Publishing: local perspectives” presentation by Sandra Joy (on a panel)

2024 “Genre Hopping” panel presentation by Alison Ferguson, John Franks, Kristen Mair (Sandra Joy moderator)

The launch

Linda Visman

I got ready early – I always do when I'm anxious – and then had to wait until a more realistic time to set off. It wouldn't look good to be too early or too eager, so, giving myself enough time for the trip, and a little extra in case of hold-ups, I set off for the centre of town.

I got off the bus a block before I needed to so I could walk, trying to settle the butterflies that were stirring up a tornado in my belly. I thought about the ordeal to come. Would everything be ready? Had my publisher arranged the launch of my first book as if he cared? How many people would turn up? What would they say about this volume that represented four years of my life? Four years of toil and doubts, of highs and lows, of going without extras so that I could spend the maximum amount of time working on my book and the minimum on other employment.

I approached the building with trepidation. The door to the conference room was open, but I could see no one. I entered the room warily and drew in my breath. James had done a wonderful job of setting up the display. On the walls around the room, posters, printed with giant representations of my book cover, advertised the first publication of a promising and talented new writer. Other decorations around the room reflected the theme of the book. It all looked great. On a large table towards the back of the room were stacked a couple of dozen books. My books! Ready for me to sign for anyone who wanted to purchase one. I wondered how many that would be.

The table where I would sit to do the signing was a lovely Queen Ann writing desk with matching chair. On it sat a leather-covered writing set, beside it was - yes, a fountain pen.

I hadn't used a fountain pen in years. I hoped the nib worked properly. Plates of finger food and champagne glasses stood on a side table, while ice buckets held unopened bottles.

Looks promising. At least James thinks there'll be a good crowd.

I walked over to where the books were stacked and picked up a copy. I tried to look at it dispassionately, as if seeing it for the first time and having no idea what it was about. The cover was simple. A photo of an old stone house took up most of the front cover, the same picture that was on the posters around the room. The title, *139 Roe Greave*, consisted of the number 139 on a brass plaque on the house door, and *Roe Greave* on a road sign that had been superimposed below the number. My name, my pen name not my real one, was modestly written below the title.

My name on my book.

The description on the back cover was realistic, giving a reasonable idea of the book's theme. It was set in the early twentieth century, in the town where I had been born. Under the blurb were a couple of excerpts from pre-launch book reviews – the best ones of course. Emotion welled up. I couldn't be dispassionate about this – I'd worked at it too hard and too long!

Just then, James entered the room.

"Ah, here's our talented author!"

Three people followed him into the room. They smiled and made encouraging noises as I was introduced to them. I turned towards the main door and saw that other guests had arrived. James went to greet them, beckoning me to follow him so that he could introduce me.

As more people arrived, the room became noisier. Waiters appeared and filled champagne glasses, carrying them around on trays. Others carried around the canapés.

The buzz of voices became louder, and it became difficult to hear the names of the people to whom I was being introduced.

James broke off the personal introductions, led me over to the main book table and picked up a small bell. Its clear sound broke through the chatter, which gradually diminished. James introduced me to the crowd.

This was the time I had been dreading. What would he say about me? How would I appear to these people who had taken the time to come and meet a new writer, of whom most had heard very little?

As James spoke I relaxed a little. He didn't use flowery language, but spoke simply and to the point. He presented a little of my background, mentioned the theme of the book and praised its cover. He then invited me to tell how I had come to write it, and what I hoped readers would take from it. I am a writer, not an orator, but I think I did pretty well. At least I didn't get booed, and they did laugh at the places they were supposed to. But I was glad when that part was over and the next part began.

As the book signing got into a rhythm, it was obvious I needn't have been concerned about how my book would be received. Several of those there had received advance copies, and had read the book.

As they came to my table to have their copies signed, they gave me their impressions of the story. Those who weren't gushy were mostly constructive in their comments, and I was feeling pretty pleased with myself.

But I'd relaxed too soon. A man approached the table as if to have a copy signed, but there was no copy in his hand. I'd noticed him earlier. He'd joined the line then abruptly walked away, only to rejoin it a few minutes later. Nervous fingers constantly pulled at his tie and his thick white hair was in disarray. He appeared unable to stand still, as if some strong emotion were struggling to escape his control. When at last he stood in front of me, I looked up and smiled at him. I asked if he wished to purchase a book so I could sign it for him. He stared at me for a few seconds without speaking, and the hatred in those grey eyes shocked me.

"I don't want your damned book!"

His voice was harsh but loud. He bent his stocky body towards me and thrust his red and sweating face close to mine. I jerked back in my chair. My heart lurched, and I know my jaw must have dropped and my eyes widened. My pleasant feelings shattered like glass.

"It's a lie. It's all a lie!" He was almost shouting. "That's not how it happened. My father was there and he told me what those other bastards really did. It wasn't like you say, the others were the ones who caused all the trouble, not my Dad and his mates. Your book blackens his name. And all the others who were there! You don't know what you're on about. I'm going to tell everyone that, just see if I don't!"

With that, he swept out a tweed-clad arm and dashed the remaining books to the floor. I jumped to my feet and stumbled backwards, afraid he was going to attack me next.

"You'll be sorry you told those lies!"

He slammed a fist on the table and spun away, evading the grasp of a couple of men composed enough to come to my assistance. Striding off, he pushed aside anyone not quick enough to get out of his way. At the door he paused and looked back. His rasping voice reached my ears.

"You'll be sorry!"

When he'd gone, everyone spoke at once, the hush that had descended over the room suddenly broken. I was aware of many curious eyes upon me and could almost hear people's thoughts.

Who is that man? What's in this book that can stir up such emotion?

I got through the rest of the evening as best I could. James soothed me, and others expressed their dismay at what had happened. My confidence had taken a battering, and my doubts about the wisdom of writing this story returned. Perhaps, even after seventy years, it was still too soon to write of the things that had occurred in my grandfather's time; things that had remained hidden for so long, which, through patient ferreting, I'd unearthed. I had written a novel, but it was based on fact. Obviously, those facts were still strongly contested by some.

One thing eased my mind. It looked like the old man's outburst had done me a favour. By the end of the evening every copy of my book had sold.

The history of the Alice Sinclair Memorial Writing Competition

Pam Garfoot

Competitions seem to be the stuff of writing groups. They are a test of the skills and artistry of everyone who enters. Those who have been awarded prizes or commendations in competitions will attest to the excitement they have felt when their work receives accolades, and those running competitions feel pride when a successful writing competition is held. In that respect, the Lake Macquarie Branch of FAW has been no different to other groups, having run a competition for over twenty years. Back in 2003 the group had been in existence for little more than two years when the very first Alice Sinclair Competition was held.

Our group's first writing competition was very much a heartfelt response to the death of respected President, Alice Sinclair. Alice had joined the group after previously being a member of the Hunter FAW. She had become the second president of the branch and led the group from mid-2001 until her untimely death in March 2003. Some of her particular strengths – ones that earned her the high regard of her branch colleagues – had been her insightful and generous critique comments and her encouraging approach to members. Soon after her death a small in-house writing competition was conceived in her honour with a single prize of $25 up for grabs. Short stories were to be no longer than 500 words and poems no more than 24 lines. Lesley Daglish was the judge for that 2003 competition and the prize winner was announced as Nola McCarthy, none other than the newly elected branch President.

Discussion amongst the group supported the idea that the in-house competition should continue. In July of 2005 judge Mel Davies presented prizes to the winners of the 2005 competition at the Annual General Meeting (prize winners for this and other years are listed below).

In the following years, much discussion was devoted to refining how the competition should be run: the terms of future competitions, proposals for potential judges, the size of the prize pool, and whether it would be limited to in-house entrants only. The longer-term features of the competition were gradually forming.

In 2008, a desire to draw a greater pool of entrants saw the scope of the competition widened to allow entrants from FAW groups in Lake Macquarie, Port Stephens, Hunter and eventually the Central Coast. Short Story and Poetry categories were included and there was an open theme. The prize pool included the princely sums of $50 for 1st prize, $30 for 2nd prize, and $20 for 3rd prize. At first entries came in very slowly, despite the widened scope, but with dogged promotion by committee members 23 entries (9 poetry, 14 short story) were received by competition closure on February 29. Pat Lindsay was the judge for that competition.

The competition, henceforth known officially as the Alice Sinclair Memorial Writing Competition, was to be held biennially from this point on. In 2010 entry was again limited to FAW members from the local area, but the word limit for short stories was set at 2,500 words and the line limit for poetry at 50 lines. The blind judging (where entrants are unknown to the judge) was done by Anna Scott. The Lake Macquarie branch did rather well, receiving a Highly Commended in the Poetry Category, and a first prize and Highly Commended in the Short Story Category.

In 2012 we saw the first competition open to all FAW members across Australia. However, numbers of entries continued to be modest (12 in all). Judges in 2012 (and again in 2014) were former members Jo Tregellis and Gail

Hennessy. Perhaps it was the low entry numbers which prompted a widening of scope in 2014: open entry and a small increase in prize money for the winning entry.

In 2016 the leap into online payment of entry fees was made and a wider publicity program conducted, resulting in a significant increase in entry numbers (23 in the Poetry Category and 45 in the Short Story Category). Indeed, although making a profit has never been the focus of the group's competition, online payment and the increased number of entries has resulted in a gradual increase in profit. That is, the income from entry fees has gradually outweighed the cost of the prize pool and other expenses involved in convening the competition. Between 2016 and 2022 profits grew steadily.

The judging panel in 2016 consisted of two judges entirely independent of the FAW, Ed Wright (a local poet) and Karen Crofts (Director of the Hunter Writers Centre at that time). From this competition onwards, entry numbers began to rise slowly and awareness of the competition grew. A stable judging panel (accomplished local writers Magdalena Ball and Jenny Blackford) for three successive competitions also helped to standardise practices and cement the reputation of the competition.

By the 2022 competition, entries had increased to 208 in total (88 in the Poetry Category and 120 in the Short Story Category). A selection of the short-listed entries in the competition was published in our group's second anthology, *Out of the shadows*. Judging the large number of entries was not for the faint-hearted, as was the job of convening the competition. The members who volunteer for the role have done marvellous jobs keeping things running smoothly behind the scenes.

Although 2024 was the next year in which a competition would normally have been held, the Committee decided to defer it until 2025 to coincide with the 25th anniversary of the Lake Macquarie FAW. It is hoped that it will be as successful as past ones and will continue the trend of gradual growth in competition standing – indeed, remaining a competition Alice Sinclair would have been proud of.

Alice Sinclair Memorial Writing Competition prize winners

2003
1st Nola McCarthy

2005
1st Wendy Alexander
1st Mel Sommers
1st Tony Mays

2008
Poetry:
1st Patricia Withers
2nd Linda Visman 'Rivers of life'
Commended Marie Every-Burns 'Autumn'

Short Story:
1st Gail Hennessy 'Morphing at the ocean baths'
2nd Lesley Mansfield 'Where are my keys'
Commended Linda Brooks 'The legacy'

2010
Poetry:
1st Patricia Withers 'Swimming pool'
2nd Eve Gray 'Mrs Aeneas Gunn is taking tea'
Commended Rina Robinson 'Mr Smith'

Short Story:
1st Linda Visman 'Black and white'
2nd Julie Simpson 'Teasing the wool of love'
Commended Linda Brooks 'Mum always said'

2012
Poetry:
1st Eve Gray 'The basket'
Commended Patricia Withers 'A birdseye view'

Short Story:
1st Victoria Norton 'Brown boxes'
2nd Mike Woodhouse 'The wages of sin'
Commended Janice Foster 'Inheritance'

2014

Poetry:

1st Jennie Herera 'A dark car awaits'

2nd Edith Speers 'The most likely person'

Commended David Berger 'Edith the cat', Bernard Russell-Smith 'Sheriff of Dawes Point', and Sheila Drakely 'The caretaker'

Short Story:

1st Claire Bell 'Ambrose, my brother dead before his time'

2nd Gavin Austin 'Leaving'

Commended Peter Miller 'A hypochondriac on the 9.24 to Central'

2016

Poetry:

1st Hessom Razavi 'Dreams'

2nd Pippa Kay 'Polio'

Commended Hessom Razavi 'Ghost'

Short Story:

1st Ryan Grice 'Borderlines'
Megan McGrath 'Tell tale'

2nd Kristen Mair 'The slow process of decay'

Commended Jan Mitchell 'Clown face', Graham McDonald 'The recycler'

2018

Poetry:

1st Anne Casey 'If I were to tell you'

2nd Linda Visman 'Tosca, Northern Territory'

Commended Kate Maxwell 'Smoke'

Short Story:

1st Linda Carter 'A handful of gravel, the click of a key'

2nd Sean Crawley 'Fishtailing'

Commended Paulette Smythe 'How to spot a bruise in a diamond crown', Brenda Madden 'Still night', Jan Mitchell 'Tony is angry'

2020

Poetry:

1st Kathryn Fry 'About the Centre, even now'
2nd Nicole Rain Sellers 'Grace'
Commended Gail Galloway 'Two crows',
Scott-Patrick Mitchell 'The morning star',

Short Story:

1st David Spitzkowsky 'Aunty'
2nd Ru Bee Chung 'Ghost'
Commended Terence Phillips 'Eileen',
Kate Murdoch 'The bonfire'

2022

Poetry:

1st Janice Williams 'Boy with a trumpet'
2nd Kathryn Fry 'The old sand mining site'
Commended Gideon McDonald 'Between the speckled lights'

Short Story:

1st Marc Canella 'Distant fires'
2nd Ned Stephenson 'Son of Prometheus'
Commended Roslyn Varley 'Ghosts',
Edith Speers 'The Flying Fortuna Sister'

Mr Popperwell takes the lead

Ned Stephenson

Winner Sydney Hammond
Short Story Competition 2023

Today's magistrate loathes me. I know because when he looks at my tie, his lip curls as though something's off in the room. I'm sure he recalls buying a car from me years ago. The giveaway is his vengeful look cloaked beneath woolly undomesticated eyebrows.

"For Mr Ternan, I award the house in Beecroft and the flat in Gordon," the magistrate says, while simultaneously smiling and frowning like an overripe Persian cat. "And of the share in the company formerly owned between the parties, he receives forty percent."

I feel the toothpick drop from my mouth.

He then sneers in my direction, to finish with, "While the remaining six properties and company share goes to the former Mrs Ternan. I distribute all other goods and chattels in accordance with the lists submitted by their counsels. Good day to you both."

Twenty-four years of marriage, six cars, two businesses, and one phantom miscarriage later, I'm left with four million dollars. While the ex-Mrs Ternan, née Codpiece, grins out of the courthouse with a hefty nine point eight million stuffed in her Gucci bag. It would have been ten big ones if she hadn't spent two hundred grand on the best divorce lawyer in town. Whereas I picked a mate's mate who owed him a favour and got a tenth of the fee and a third of the assets. Nicely played, Bill, you idiot.

~

Outside the district courthouse, the ex-Mrs Ternan, née Pesticide, marches up with her yeasty bulldog. The snorting, slobbering fellow looks like his face is about to implode. How the lad can take a dump with legs built like question marks is beyond me.

"Here!" A tentacle thrusts out the dog lead.

"Here what?"

"Mr Popperwell is yours."

"But I don't want the dog."

"You should have read the lists better."

Mr Popperwell sniffs my leg as though he's never met me before. Even with his forehead pressed against my trouser leg, his nose is still an inch from the fabric.

"But ... I don't want the dog. He's yours."

"Not anymore. I have a new Lowchen x Cavalier King Charles puppy."

The ex-Mrs Ternan, née Tapeworm, drops the lead at my feet and strides off before I can speak. It's at this moment, as the magistrate materialises like a patrol cop in a school zone, Mr Popperwell proves me wrong by showing the world he has no trouble shitting. The crusty old judge gives me the pick that up face he's undoubtedly given countless poor dog owners before me.

Of course, the darling hangs around to make sure, doesn't he? I scan the street for a plastic bag. There's nothing. The best I can do is dig out my clean hanky.

The turd is huge and hot, and moisture seeps through the material before I reach the bin.

~

After a few false starts trying to get Mr Popperwell into the car, and with my hand pressed firmly against an old hernia scar, the new bachelors set off home. It takes three suburbs to realise we're driving the wrong way. Palm Beach isn't mine now. Bugger that woman; there's a better pub and even better Indian takeaway around the corner from the Gordon flat.

"What do you think, Mr Popperwell? How's this for a blessed change?" I say aloud.

Mr Popperwell is smearing his face against the passenger's side window like a kid painting with snails. Something from his nose has left black lines across the glass.

"You want some air? Gees, you don't half pong. Didn't Mrs Chlamydia ever wash you?"

On cue, he turns to me and farts wetly into the faux leather seat. I drop both windows, which creates a vortex of warm tar, diesel exhausts, and abattoir haze.

"God Almighty! What've you been eating?"

Mr Popperwell has the good grace to begin panting.

"I've never been one for following rules," I say with my arm across my face. "My view on life is if you come to a fork in the road, always turn left. You with me, buddy?"

Mr Popperwell doesn't like the windows down. He takes to licking his balls, which comes as a surprise as I thought the ex-Mrs Ternan, née Formaldehyde, had neutered the poor sod. She'd made damn sure I'd been nutted before our first anniversary ticked over.

~

By my third beer, the pub's wooden chair has become bearable, and my bachelor-in-arms is asleep with his head against my suede loafers. He enjoyed his saucer of Melbourne Bitter although clearly hasn't the head for beer. The great lump must weigh thirty kilos, so I figured he could handle a whole can without breaking a sweat, but to be fair, he's had a big day. Mr Popperwell wheezes gently as I scratch behind his ear.

“Hello handsome man!” says a woman out of nowhere.

“You referring to me or him?”

The mid-thirties woman reaches down to pat my dog. “I love it when owners and their pets look alike.”

Being compared to an overweight bulldog would normally bring me to my feet, but when said by a girl with a smile like daylight and a chest you could rest your head on, instead, I automatically grin back.

“Would you like a drink?” I boldly ask.

“That would be lovely.” She takes a seat opposite me as Mr Popperwell grunts over so he can snuffle his dribbly chops against her outstretched palm.

“I have a bulldog as well,” she says.

“You do?”

“Miss Mansfield’s her name. I think she’d like your manly boy here.”

Mr Popperwell starts making obscene noises into the hand of this poor woman.

“She would?”

The woman points to my pint glass. “I’ll have what you’re having.”

I stand to get my new friend a drink, and with a ray of sunshine returning, begin my fourth trip to the bar for the day, while behind me Mr Popperwell rudely embraces a stockinged leg.

Writing competitions: should I enter them?

Linda Visman

Do you ever wonder if entering competitions is worthwhile? Even seasoned writers have different opinions – it depends upon their experiences. Some say it is not worth the time, effort and cost of entering. Others say entering competitions has been of great benefit to them. It is a good idea to look at the benefits of entering competitions – and any problems to be aware of if you do.

Entering competitions can:

Provide inspiration.

Sometimes, you just don't know what to write about and are seeking new ideas. I can speak from experience here.

Some years ago, I entered an online short story competition that required entrants to write to a prompt. I was so inspired by the prompt that I wrote not one but eight related stories, all in a week. My usual output at the time was a couple of stories a month.

Caution: Some competitions are so bland it is hard to be inspired by them. Choose wisely. There are many online sites that provide guides to legitimate competitions.

Provide motivation.

There are times when I cannot write. I feel like my well of creativity has dried up, so I don't write. Then I may see an interesting competition and make myself write for it. Even if I don't enter, I have achieved something. I have written, and it is only writing that breaks the so-called "writer's block".

Caution: Choose the right ones to enter.

Provide a challenge.

Competitions can inspire you to stretch yourself – to write in different genres or forms, or about unusual themes. They can develop your style and keep your writing fresh. The competition I mentioned earlier meant writing fantasy stories. I had never written fantasy, but the prompt stirred my creativity and challenged me to write in a genre I was unfamiliar with.

Caution: Look for competitions that test you; many don't.

Provide a learning experience.

If you are open to constructive criticism, it can at least lead to great improvements in your writing technique. Unfortunately, many competitions do not provide feedback, but those that do can be of great assistance in pointing out strengths and weaknesses and suggesting options.

Meeting a challenge can lead to learning more about the writing process and, if you write about something new to you, your knowledge of that topic is increased as well.

As a new writer wary of high standards, you can begin by entering small, local affairs, and gradually work your way up to the larger and more prestigious ones.

Caution: The value of feedback, if provided, depends on the knowledge, skill and insight of the judge/s. They can give you great help and inspiration or be completely useless. It helps to know the preferences of the judges too, as they, like all of us, carry biases towards certain kinds of writing.

Provide discipline.

Competitions usually come with rules, or strict guidelines relating to topic, length, genre, style, format, deadlines, etc. Staying within a certain framework can be of great benefit. For example, word limits encourage you to keep your writing taut, and deadlines force you to write when you may not feel like it.

Caution: No real negatives here.

Build your portfolio or CV.

In some competitions, winning or being placed results in publication, in a magazine or anthology, an e-zine or website. Every publication is another proof of your writing ability. Even competitions that don't result in publication add to your CV.

Caution: The more respected the competition, the more it will mean. You may want to start with lesser-known ones, become familiar with their requirements, and work up.

Launch your writing career.

Success in reputable competitions gets your name out there, perhaps even attracting publishers' attention. Many well-known authors started by entering writing competitions.

Caution: You need to be successful in the right ones and, in those, you face stiff competition.

Earn you money.

While most competitions pay little, if anything, for a win or place, some can bring in reasonable money.

Caution: You usually have to pay to enter, and some are not worth the outlay. Entry fees should be low and the prizes a lot higher. In many instances, you are competing against a large number of very good writers.

So, is it worth it to enter?

Only you can decide that. Work out your motivations for entering. Keep in mind the points above and see if there is anything in it for you. Then decide.

Things to remember

Having your writing critiqued by fellow writers is a great way to make sure your item is worthy of entering into a competition. They can help you iron out any problems that may have escaped you.

If you do enter one, always make sure you follow the rules, present quality work, and use the results to continually improve your writing. Good luck!

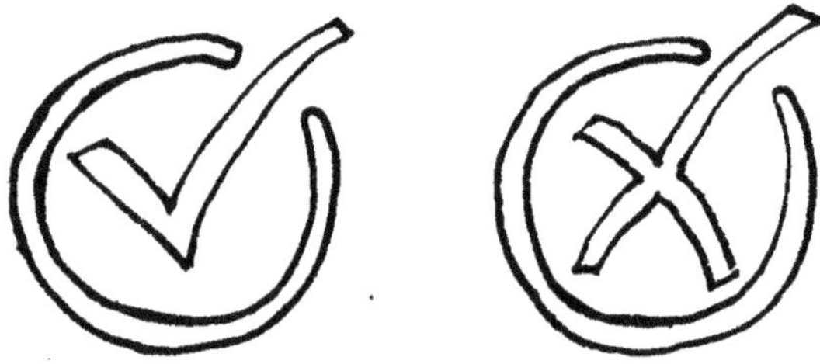

Write Here! Festival 2024

Alison Ferguson

Literary festivals are an important event on any writer's calendar. Some festivals focus more on literary than commercial fiction, while others are designed with the reader (ie. the book buyer!) in mind. One festival that aims to support our local community of writers is the annual 'Write Here' Festival.

Lake Macquarie libraries have been holding the 'Write Here' Festival for a number of years with the aim of showcasing the work of local and visiting authors. Their programs have included book launches, panel presentations, and writing workshops across a wide range of genres and these have proved ideal for supporting the work of emerging authors and local readers. The Festival organisers do their best to keep the cost of attending to a minimum, with the support from the Lake Macquarie Council. For example, many sessions are offered free of charge or by gold coin donation only.

Naturally, many of our branch members regularly attend this festival to participate in the audience as well as to present. If the idea of facing an audience to talk about writing is new to you, then this is an ideal festival in which to participate, either as an individual or with other branch members. The venues are small (usually one of the local libraries), and the audiences are friendly and will include your cheer squad of family, friends and fellow branch members.

Additionally, we like to provide the opportunity for a practice run at one of our branch meetings so you can iron out any knotty spots in the presentation.

In May 2024, Sandra Boyd chaired a panel on the topic of 'Genre Hopping' which explored the different categories of writing which provide readers (and writers) with a guide to the content and structure of the written work. I was one of the panel along with John Franks, and Kristen Mair. My transition from academic writing to historical fiction writing has ended up in my current writing as science fiction. John was able to draw upon his experience of writing his recently published novel *Echoes* which alternated historical fiction with a present-day story which, to his own surprise, ended up with 'romantic elements'. Kristen drew on her screenwriting course to unpack some of the key structural elements that differ across genres.

As always, the audience was lively and asked perceptive questions that sharpened everybody's attention to the facets of quality writing and what it provides to the reader. This is a festival that is definitely worth your time!

Cate, Tony, Pam and Linda at 2019 Write Here Festival, Toronto Library

Section 5

When we write

Writing isn't just a scheduled activity – it's part of our rhythm. Beyond formal meetings, we write together weekly, often with coffee in hand, making creativity a habit and finding support in consistency and community.

Christmas parties, a historical reflection

George Graves

Many, many years ago I sat on the edge of the verandah at Jan's place. There were about twenty people there at the house, relaxing on a variety of chairs, with a few tables nearby groaning under the weight of the food. It was the first time I had been to a Christmas party with the writers group. It was so much fun.

The food was enjoyable – a mixture of varieties that people brought with them. However, that was not the most memorable aspect. Food, for me, is not the most important thing in my life. It is something to have at certain times of the day.

What did I enjoy? What was so memorable? It was the play acting. There were poems. And short stories. Really short stories, not some long-winded tomes, that drifted over the gathering. They were fun. Not serious ones. Not one was like that. And a play about the seven deadly sins. At least, after all these passing years, with lots of uncertainty, I think that was what it was about.

They were all very light-hearted and so cleverly written and presented. It was just what I needed on that day.

I felt I was included and part of the group. And so, I was encouraged to keep on jotting down some short stories and poems for others in the group to look at. To take them to what is called a critique group.

Christmas parties since then have been held in a variety of places. At all of them, there was some entertainment. We have had stories about Christmas, short stories that had nothing to do with Christmas, music, Christmas trees, jokes about Christmas to the groans of the audience, and much more.

The food has always been enjoyable, with people bringing food to share with others. Of course, during the years of peak Covid, each person ate the meal they brought with them.

What was the best part of these parties? The food? The entertainment? The venue? No. For me, it was the people. They made it enjoyable, fun and memorable.

Various Christmas celebrations at George's and Jan's.

The January social meeting, a historical reflection

Pam Garfoot

Aside from the excessive heat of a Lake Macquarie summer, January can often be a quiet month. Christmas is over and things calm down. That's why it's our tradition to get together, mid-January, for a social lunch. No pressure: just a bring-your-own lunch with, perhaps, a sweet treat to share. We usually meet at the home of one of our members, so our January social gathering is beautifully relaxed.

We do make some concessions to the fact that we are writers. Each member takes a turn to speak briefly about their writing achievements for the year that has just ended – what they managed to do, what they didn't get done, what they are proud of.

Next each member talks about their writing goals for the forthcoming year, trying to keep those goals SMART (specific, measurable, achievable, realistic, timely). Sometimes we even write the goals down and seal them in an envelope to be reviewed at the gathering next year. Even though many goals go unachieved, articulating them helps us to make progress on our dreams.

Some years our January social includes some writerly entertainment – a poem or a quick story perhaps. One memorable January we even enjoyed a fun performance in costume to accompany one of Tony's humorous poems.

Starting the year with a relaxed social gathering helps, I think, in bringing us together as a group and in getting us to focus on where we are going as writers.

Janary Social Gatherings at George's home.

General meetings: how we learn about good writing and what it achieves

Pam Garfoot

From the earliest days of our group the Committee was convinced of the need to offer presentations, workshops and focused discussions which would educate members and help them become better writers. Over the years much effort has been put into the process of planning sessions with talented external speakers or with members who could share their expertise and experience.

Even the most experienced of our members benefit from hearing from great speakers, and there's no doubt we've had many. At each general meeting, we also usually include a short writing exercise, and these help all members to keep honing their skills. Indeed, many of the short pieces produced through writing exercises have ended up forming the basis of wonderful short stories.

Over the past 25 years we've explored a wide range of topics, some of which have been revisited multiple times. We've covered most writing genres and a huge array of different skills which writers should master.

In the first ten years we explored topics such as: how to give and receive feedback, travel writing, computing for writers, getting inspired to write poetry, writing articles, punctuation, playwriting, getting published, showing not telling, self-editing, dialogue, haiku, writing with the senses, writing for teenagers, memoir, internet publishing, and the list goes on.

In case that was all not enough, in the next ten years we examined characterisation, critiquing, romance writing, how to write an author biography, creativity, various grammar and technical topics, pitching, structuring your novel, writing family history, blogging, experimental fiction, imagery, fantasy writing, entering competitions, ekphrasis, point-of-view, limericks, and much more. We've even sought inspiration by taking excursions to local spots like The Old Brush and Pokolbin.

More recently, topics have been as diverse as editing and proofreading, turning a book into an audio book, writing historical non-fiction, working with a commercial publisher, writing for children, how reading leads to better writing, writers and AI , and copywriting.

We've had some fabulous writers come to our meetings to generously offer us insights into aspects of writing and their own writing journeys. Some of these have included Beverley George, Ron Vickress, Magdalena Ball, Annie West, Claire Pasvolsky, Jaye Ford, Ryan O'Neill, Jan Dean, Kaz Delaney, Lee Christine, Ed Wright, and of course our own talented members. Some presenters have been happy to talk to us multiple times - and for this we offer our grateful thanks.

Members have learnt a great deal from all our presenters. What's more, hearing from published writers about their own writing journeys has helped to inspire us and stimulate our own writing journeys.

Photo: Pam's presentation to the general meeting on Writing Microlit, 10 Aug 2019

What else do we gain?
FRIENDS

Poem

Rob West

Falling rusty leaves
Cover young shoots from freezing
Throughout winter's chill

Section 6

Where we write

We may dream of forest cabins, but our real writing happens in kitchens, cafes, and borrowed corners. This section reflects on the spaces that hold our words – and where we imagine our writing will take us next.

Places we've met

Pam Garfoot

Our group had barely begun twenty-five years ago before we began to meet regularly, in rented premises, in what seemed the most central part of Lake Macquarie – the pretty lakeside town of Toronto. The Toronto Multi-Purpose Centre (in Thorne Street, Toronto) became the venue for our meetings. In 2016 we moved our general meetings to the Toronto Library meeting room. However, the library space proved too small for our growing group and, a year later, we moved to The HUB (located in the upper part of The Boulevard in Toronto). Two years later, in 2019, we moved back to the Toronto Multi-Purpose Centre where we have remained since.

As other meetings usually attract fewer participants, they have often been held elsewhere. Over the years several members have generously offered their homes (in places like Wangi, Buttaba, Rathmines, Kilaben Bay) for critique and Committee meetings. We've also had regular critique meetings at the Rathmines Bowling Club and the Wangi Workers Club. Luckily, our local area has many beautiful locations to offer us.

From time to time, we have made excursions to more far-flung places like The Old Brush (in Brunkerville, NSW) and Pokolbin (in the Hunter Valley). Such excursions are always fun, offering us new inspirations for our writing.

Toronto Multi-Purpose Centre

The HUB

Toronto Library

Anywhere!

But where do the individuals go to write?

In hospital whilst receiving chemotherapy

Coffee shop / cafes, with lots of coffee

Public transport (train, bus, tram)

Boat or train, here or overseas

Bookshops with seating

Home office or study

University campus

Coworker's space

Kitchen table

Museum

Beach

Hotel

Library

Forest cabin

Art gallery café

Parks and gardens

Zoo or aquarium café

Train station waiting room

Botanic gardens glasshouse

Car (parked, or as a passenger), or on the window

Caption: LADIES OF THE LAKE: Authors Linda Visman, Magdalena Ball and Jaye Ford. *Picture: Phil Hearne.*

The Convent, Pokolbin

An alarming meeting

Alison Ferguson

The sunblasted streets were empty. Behind drawn blinds, residents had retreated from the heat, lying prostrate before their air-conditioning units and praying to the gods of the old coal-fired energy station for the power to stay on.

As we gathered for our regular general meeting in the multi-purpose centre, we too cranked up the fans to the max, sending them into a frenzied snickersee above our heads. The guest speaker was introduced and began to drone about the elegant distinctions between the subjunctive and conditional moods. Eyelids drooped and heads began to nod with the weight of his arguments. It was shaping up to be a long meeting.

Whoop, whoop. The rising wail of the fire alarm jolted us awake.

Whoop, whoop. Louder and louder the alarms sounded through the empty hall. The guest speaker lost his grip on his notes. The pages fell to the floor. He scanned our faces for help.

Whoooop! An automated voice commanded, 'Evacuate the building. Evacuate the building.'

We looked to each other. The alarm had never gone off before and, having organised this talk, none of the committee had girded their grammatical loins to attend.

Two of our older members had already cranked themselves upright, grabbed their walkers, and were half-way to the door. No one bothered to look about for any signs of smoke. Instead we too shuffled after them to the door and gathered in the car park where the whoop of the alarm mercifully faded enough to allow conversation.

The consensus of opinion was that fire engines would come. Surely a community centre's alarm would set off an automatic response at the fire station? Our guest speaker offered to continue his talk but his offer was quickly and unanimously suppressed.

Lucky were those with walkers who could perch on their flip up seats. The rest of us could feel the baking asphalt melting the soles of our shoes. One enterprising member thought to check the contact information listed on the side of the front door and began to ring all of the numbers listed. Three numbers rang out without an answer, while two clicked straight over to voice mail.

Despair and dehydration were a powerful combination. Half the group left, seeking the air-conditioned relief of their homes. A hardy few of us remained until the alarm began to wind down, unattended, and unmourned. Then we went home too.

However, the thing about our general meetings is there is always something to learn. On that occasion, the grammatical lesson I learned was that if a fire occurs then the alarm could sound (conditional mood), and if it were to happen again then I would not hang about waiting (subjunctive mood).

The road to Gunnedah

Tony Lang

There's some folk walking back
On a long-forgotten track
On the road to Gunnedah.
They were heading for 'The Brush'
But they didn't know the way
So the driver kept on driving
But then heard someone say,
"Stop the car, O Linda,
I think we've gone too far
We're on the road to Gunnedah!"

So they had a little meet
In Breeza's only street
Along the road to Gunnedah.
Linda had a GPS,
They thought they'd be OK
But the flamin' thing was broken
And it took them far away
In their car, off the tar
To the township of Coolah,
Way out past Gunnedah.

So they turned the car around,
They'd covered so much ground
Some miles from Gunnedah.
Then Linda put her foot down,
They'd many miles to do,
But the sun was in her eyes
And that's when they hit the 'roo.
With no sump or water pump
Their swags they had to hump
On the road to Gunnedah.

So if you see some dusty tramps
With blisters and with cramps
On the road to Gunnedah,
Just chuck them in the boot
Of your Holden car or ute,
For they're hungry and they're thirsty
And they're very sore of foot.
As you gently set them down
In old Toronto town
Don't mention "Brush" or Gunnedah!

This is a fictional story.

Historical Fact:

A few years ago, members of the LMFAW decided to have a day of writing and learning at "The Old Brush" not far from Mulbring. Unfortunately, not all got there. One carload got lost on the way. This is a true story but it wasn't ME!!...

Finding my writing home

Cate Plink

From early childhood I spent hours, mostly when I should be doing something else, but also in bed at night, telling myself stories. I was an avid reader, so those early stories were mostly adaptations of other writers' stories with myself as the heroine. I certainly didn't think of writing stories at three or four, but I was certainly making them up in my head. Sometimes when things were hard, I would lie awake for hours making up a pretend life for myself.

As I grew older the internal stories became more complex, but I still never thought that I might one day be an author. Famous people were authors, not people like me. I had, well still have I suppose, a habit of reading a story, then re-doing it in my own mind, trying to make it a better story. One day I was reading a romance story, and I got so mad at the silliness of it, I threw the book across the room saying, "I could write a better story than that."

"Well, why don't you?" My husband said, picking up the book that he had dodged, and handing it back to me.

Those words started me on a long, long journey. In my spare time I would try to write down and make proper stories of the ones that had been inside my head for most of my life. I started many and finished none. I lost faith in myself many times but couldn't stop trying. I did creative writing courses, screen writing courses, and even poetry courses, but still struggled to find the spark that turns a simple idea into a fully-fledged book.

One day, in 1994, a friend saw some of the writing my youngest son had done for school and invited me to take him to a special meeting of a branch of the FAW, where local youngsters were going to present some of their work. I was impressed by what the branch did and ended up joining on my own behalf.

Over the next twelve years, I was in and out of the FAW. I moved several times and tried two or three other branches that were closer at that time but returned to the first one in the end. I enjoyed the meetings, and in 2009 became the delegate to the State Council for that branch and ended up on the State Committee. My writing improved through the help of the branch, but there was still something not good enough in my work. In the meantime, notebook after notebook continued to stuff the drawers and shelves in my room, already filled with stories that went nowhere.

It took me a long time to realise what the problem was. Each time a piece was read out in a meeting, the members would praise the work effusively, and offer helpful hints, but little in the way of genuine critique, and it was this critique that I needed to help me improve my work.

By the time I moved to the coast in early 2011, I had manuscripts for two full novels, both of which had been turned down by mainstream publishing. I had also been badly burned by so-called publishing places which took thousands of dollars for no return. I remained in the FAW, enjoying my role as the Competition Secretary, which I still find rewarding. Although the branch I joined when I moved offered much better critiquing, I was still struggling.

In 2016 I found Lake Macquarie FAW which had two critique meetings each month separate from the general meetings. This meant that more time was given to a full assessment of the piece. Also, having the piece read by somebody other than yourself gives you a much better insight into where problems lie. The critiquing is intense, and sometimes difficult for the writer to hear, although always done in a kind way. It is critique you receive, not criticism. Also, the general meetings always have interesting, challenging workshops which are great aids to improving your writing.

Within a few months of these meetings, I found myself rewriting the two finished novels and I received good critique for them. They have been now independently published by somebody I fully trust, and I hope to have the next one out soon. Not only that, with LMFAW I found true friends who care about and support each other. I have found my true writing home.

Speaking from the perspective of the Vice President of FAW(NSW) State Committee, what I have found at LMFAW is a branch that fully embodies all the aims of an organisation that was established in 1928 to try and fulfill the dream of Henry Lawson to promote writing in Australia.

In search of inspiration

Alison Ferguson

In May 2017, we hired a minibus and headed out in search of fresh ideas to a familiar neck of the woods, the Hunter Valley Vineyards. We explored The Convent, Constable Estate, Drayton's Family Estate and the windy heights for views of the valley, refreshed by coffee and (just a few) wine tastings. We may even have penned a few lines.

Keeping costs to a minimum we managed to snaffle a rackety old minibus and driver for $20 a head for twelve of us in the middle of the week. We threw an esky in the back filled with water and snacks and headed out of town at 9.30 in the morning (also known as 'the crack of dawn' to many members). Naturally, coffee was a priority so our first stop was the café at The Convent in Pokolbin. As we wandered about the gardens of this historic building, it was easy to imagine the lives of the Brigidine order of nuns who once lived there.

We dropped in to the Constable Estate Vineyards just up the road, which was closed in 2023 (due to the passing of owner, David Constable). Ten minutes later we were battling high winds at the top of a hill, trying to open our packed lunches. Lunch over, we scuttled back to Drayton's Family Wines for coffee and other warming drinks. Once there, we settled down for a writing bee. What we wrote seems to have been lost in time (or alcohol), but I do still cherish the quick portrait of me done by Pam Garfoot – she's really caught the concentration!

Finally, there was some singing on the bus on the way home – so by the end of the afternoon, we'd paid homage to all the muses and awaited inspiration in due course.

Our minibus to Pokolbin

At the convent

Alison, a sketch by Pam Garfoot 3/5/2017

Elizabeth, Constable Estate

The chocolate shop, a memory

George Graves

"Poor old codger. Is he losing it a bit?"

I don't think that would have come to my friend's mind at all. Not at all. Well, I hope not!

I had just read out the story I had written about our group's finances to him. It was interesting hearing his comments about the part where I said we went to The Chocolate Shop.

"We simply did not go to a chocolate shop on the way to The Old Brush. It did not happen!"

Oh!

I remembered so many things about that shop. It seemed so real. It still seems so real!

So, why do we remember things? To say we remember things that are memorable is simply a circular argument.

I think we remember different things, or times, or people because they have an impact on us, on our emotions or on our senses at that moment.

Our memories do not have date stamps attached to them. They are not like photos on our computer or phone that, when we look them up, display the moment we took them. Oh look - that one of us was taken on the 18th of December two years ago. How about that! I thought it was longer ago.

It is the association with other memories that may bring up thoughts of places, of things, or of people. However, sometimes, just now and then, the links to the associations may become a little frayed. Perhaps that is what has happened to me.

So, I'm not sure when I visited The Chocolate Shop. But I still think I went there. Some time. With a group of friends. Many years ago.

What do I remember about the shop? Oh, the aroma. And the displays of rows and rows of different chocolates, some with swirls on top, others plain. Just so many choices of different shapes and textures.

Also, I remember the smiles of the others as they selected their favourites or something new to tantalise their taste buds. Chocolate that melted in the mouth. Ones that hinted at orange, or mint, or hazelnut or, what seemed, a thousand other flavours.

After the first chocolate, or the tenth that is popped into one's mouth, oh, the memories that drift back into our mind. The last time we might have tasted that was beside the creek, just the two of us, with the trees overhanging the water and the birds chirping nearby. Or a time on a yacht, a few miles offshore. Or at the theatre where a favourite movie was showing. Or a thousand other stories, each one important to that person.

I think it is the association of the delightful aroma and taste that may link the times and bring back the memories. I know a particular perfume will do that for me.

A few days later I read a story written by one of our group about some of the activities taken in the past. In one, a trip to the wine country at Pokolbin was mentioned. I had completely forgotten that.

And on the way there we had stopped at The Chocolate Shop!

Yea! I'm not going completely bonkers! Years and years ago, we, our group, did go to The Chocolate Shop.

I suppose the wine was not so important to me, and that is why I had forgotten that aspect of the trip. However, the chocolate did mean something to me. Yes!

Now this may come as a surprise to some but I do not eat chocolate!

But the aroma! Yes! And the smiles of friends as they selected their choices and delighted in the flavours. That will not be forgotten.

Moving forward:
where do you see LMFAW in 2050?

After a successful 25 years, members were asked, "Where do you see LMFAW in another 25 years?" Compiled by Sandra Boyd at the social gathering on 11 January 2025

Here are some of our thoughts on that day:

"Members will be microchipped with AI so that their ideas will be networked to produce creative writing."

Alison Ferguson

"Same place, same values, same inspirations."

Olga Korlevic

"I think it will be a vibrant group still, with people passionate about creative writing."

Bethany Wooden

"We will all be famous, even if some of us are ashes by then. We will all be using very advanced technology to write stories."

Emma Walton

"I think we will be in survival mode from climate change and the loss of democracy to autocratic governments."

Jan Mitchell

"I think LMFAW will be thriving along with a strong state."

Cate Plink

"I would hope that we are still using our **own** imagination to generate our stories (spell checkers are ok!); and each have a fun place to write. We will still be encouraging each other to write different styles."

George Graves

"I don't know!"

Lyn

"I don't see much in 2050. I'll either be a centenarian or dust. My pessimism is based on the fact we are an aging group and without new blood we may not exist."

John Franks

"FAW needs to appeal to younger, new members or we will be extinct."

Rob West

"With young writers coming up – there will always be writers, and always a need for mutual support. So I believe the group has great promise ahead."

Linda Visman

"It will be thriving!"

Alison Ferguson

"I think we will have a house computer that will be attached to every appliance including our computer, which will spit out anything we request."

Black Crow Walking

Moving forward: what will writing be like in 2050?

After a successful 25 years, members were asked "Writing styles and tools have changed so much. What do you think it will be like to be a writer in another 25 years?"Compiled by Sandra Boyd at the social gathering on 11 January 2025

Here are some of our thoughts on that day:

"I think writing will be null and void because AI will write for us and we won't even have to prompt it because it listens to us through our phones."

Black Crow Walking

"We will still have creative writers, but their tools will be different. Pen and paper are already almost completely done, as technology has taken over. I can see AI being important. However, I believe it will be a tool, not a source of the creative process."

Linda Visman

"Knowledge is valuable, e.g. X and Musk is now a billionaire from hoarding it. It follows that writers will be highly paid, licensed by the state and we will be in a Brave New World. AI will be the tool."

Rob West

"People will reject AI in favour of traditionally written works. Themes that were appropriate previously will not be acceptable anymore. More characters that reflect diverse backgrounds will be represented. Fiction representing diverse cultures will become popular."

Bethany Wooden

"I can't see much future in writing in its current form. It is already undergoing change, especially in style and form. Traditional aspects of present-day writing will be almost non-existent. Eg. grammar, spelling, syntax perhaps. The onset of AI will likely lead to dictating and computer programs will turn it into text in whichever style the author nominates."

John Franks

"Styles may change. Tools may be used but the ideas I hope will be generated by the individual. I hope AI is not used to make the major part of the stories. (I hope AI is not used at all, but I may not be realistic!)"

George Graves

"I think voice will play a greater role in recording and relaying stories. In that context, writing will possibly be considered an old skill. Holograms will play a greater role, and I think AI will be used more, taking depth and emotion out of books."

Cate Plink

"People will be fed up with AI and will start to compete with it. The quality of the writing will be assessed against its originality and uniqueness as opposed to the AI-generated language."

Olga Korlevic

"Charcoal sticks in the ashes – no more technologies."

Jan Mitchell

"We will be using some type of technology that's so advanced to a point that we don't even call it technology. It will be so complicated to us in this day and age but so cool and trendy with the kids of 2050. Aliens would already have been discovered and every single person in the world will be famous. All in regards to writing."

Emma Walton

The last word from the current president of LMFAW

Sandra Boyd

The written word has always been important to society. From the days of papyrus to the modern digital devices, the industry has survived many changes.

But, to have the written word, you need people who know and understand the words of their culture.

At the LMFAW, we have writers who have dedicated their lives to words; librarians, teachers, lecturers, and more. We also have writers who have finally decided to leave their written mark on the world and take the leap to authorship.

Through competitions, anthologies, publications and presentations, our writers - past and present - have given of themselves to write a message that will bring the full range of emotions to others.

The vastness of our membership means that we have members experienced in (or keen to learn about) various genres and subgenres. We have those who thrill and scare; those who make you weep for joy - or sadness; those who inspire and motivate; those who give you cause to reflect.

But, always, they write to show you that it ***can*** be done and it ***should*** be done. Your words are important.

At the January social gathering this year, I asked the members to look forward another 25 years and write where they thought the LMFAW would be, and what they thought writing would be like. Their answers were as varied as their writing styles and personalities. Then I had to think about what answers I would give.

We've seen parts of the industry threatened with Artificial Intelligence, and I don't think that's going away. The internet hadn't been available for long before people started screaming that it needed to be tamed. It was too late, and now we *can't* live without it. I think A.I. will be the same. We will push back against it, but it is here to stay - in one form or another.

I think that technology will continue to be a tool that writers use. Very few of us would be willing to write without our computers and other devices. And publishing is not an option without it.

I do, however, hope that the human mind continues to explore the world through writing and reading. I hope we endeavour to experience the world with words, and share those feelings with others who read them.

So, where will the LMFAW be in 2050? I think membership numbers will go up and down, venue hire prices will continue to rise, and time will become harder to find.

But ... I think there will still be members of this wonderful group of writers who aim to get their words out of their imaginations and share them with the world. Perhaps we will all meet in a cabin in the country.

I urge you all to write more, for it is through your words that emerging authors find the bravery to start their journey.

It is an absolute priviledge to head up this organisation. It can never be a solo role, and I thank the committee for the hours and hours of work they do in making everything run seamlessly for the members. I thank the members, for showing up, for sharing your writing and sharing of yourself.

Cheers, Sandi

www.ingramcontent.com/pod-product-compliance
Lightning Source LLC
Chambersburg PA
CBHW061101100726
47911CB00012B/338

* 9 7 8 0 6 4 6 7 2 3 6 0 0 *